TRS-80
ASSEMBLY LANGUAGE

HUBERT S. HOWE, JR.

A SPECTRUM BOOK

Prentice-Hall, Inc.
Englewood Cliffs, New Jersey 07632

Library of Congress Cataloging in Publication DATA

HOWE, HUBERT S
    TRS-80 assembly language.

    (A Spectrum Book)
    Bibliography: p. 186
    1. TRS-80 (Computer)—Programming. 2. Assembler
language (Computer program language) I. Title.
QA76.8.T18H68   001.64′2   80-20578
ISBN 0-13-931139-4
ISBN 0-13-931121-1 (pbk.)

To Stefanie

A SPECTRUM BOOK

10 9 8 7

Printed in The United States of America

Editorial/production supervision by Frank Moorman
Interior design by Dawn Stanley
Manufacturing buyer: Cathie Lenard

This book was composed using a Diablo HyType I printer with Michael Shrayer's Electric Pencil program on a TRS-80 Model I Microcomputer.

PRENTICE-HALL INTERNATIONAL, INC., London
PRENTICE-HALL OF AUSTRALIA PTY. LIMITED, Sydney
PRENTICE-HALL OF CANADA, LTD., Toronto
PRENTICE-HALL OF JAPAN, INC., Tokyo
PRENTICE-HALL OF SOUTHEAST ASIA PTE. LTD., Singapore
WHITEHALL BOOKS LIMITED, Wellington, New Zealand

TABLE OF CONTENTS

Part I: Basic Concepts

Preface

This book has grown out of a series of columns that I have been writing for over a year in the TRS-80 MONTHLY NEWS MAGAZINE (originally called the TRS-80 MONTHLY NEWSLETTER), published by H & E Computronics. Although the columns began as an attempt to explain various aspects of assembly-language programming to beginners, it gradually became clear to me that the incorporation of this material into a single volume would be more attractive and useful for most readers.

Both beginners and experienced programmers have good reason to be dissatisfied with the material on assembly-language programming that has appeared thus far. Most of it is lacking in some of the essential details that you need to know in order to understand and to use the TRS-80, and much of this literature is very poorly written. While there are some aspects of the TRS-80 that are still not covered in this book, such as details about the Level II Basic interpreter, it contains most of the information that you need to know in order to develop assembly-language programs, and the book itself presents numerous practical programs and subroutines that have been fully tested. It also includes many of those "secrets" of the ROM and the Disk Operating Systems that you need to know in order to comprehend fully what goes on inside the TRS-80.

I would like to express my gratitude to several people who have helped in the realization of this book: to Howard Gosman, publisher of the TRS-80 MONTHLY NEWS MAGAZINE, where the columns first appeared; to John Harding, who provided the encouragement needed to develop the columns into a book. Thanks also go to Emory Cook, who gave me many helpful suggestions. I am also grateful to the numerous readers who have provided both criticism and ideas for further pursuit.

Hubert S. Howe, Jr.
New City, New York

1

MACHINE LANGUAGE

1.1   What is Machine Language?

This is a book that has been written in order to explain machine language or assembly-language programming for the TRS-80 microcomputer to beginners. It is assumed that you have some familiarity with Level II Basic, and that you will have access to a TRS-80 with at least 16K memory and Level II Basic in order to try out programming ideas and examples of machine code introduced in different chapters.

If you are familiar with Basic, you are probably aware that the instructions you write in a Basic program are not the same as what the machine actually executes. Your statements are decoded in a rather complicated way, and instructions that carry out the actions you have directed the machine to perform are executed for you. Basic itself is a program called an "interpreter" that is written in the machine language of the Z-80 microprocessor, which is the heart of the TRS-80. "Machine language" refers to a program, like Basic, that is actively running inside a computer. "Assembly language" refers to another program that you run called an "assembler" that takes individual instructions written in symbolic form and converts them into machine language.

All computers execute machine language and ONLY machine language. Any other way of interacting with the computer merely involves providing data to a program running in the

1

machine.   You may never be aware of what the language is, and
for many situations it would make no difference. In general,
the higher the level of the language being employed by the
computer, the further removed it is from the machine language.
The problem with this process is that it takes longer and
longer for the computer to execute each basic operation you
specify.   The execution of one line in a Basic program may
require millions or even billions of machine operations.

     When you write a program in assembly language, you are
taking advantage of the computer's internal structure so that
what you write can be executed much more efficiently than
instructions in symbolic languages. Execution efficiency is
not the only advantage, however.   It is also true that what
the program can do may often be more extensive or elegant than
what programs in higher-level languages can do.

     The disadvantage of machine language programming is that
you have to understand the structure of the computer in detail
to get it to work for you. A single error can cause an entire
program that works in every other respect not just to
malfunction, but to do disastrous things like erase itself
from memory.   Machine-language programming can be messy,
requiring that you remember what is happening within every
single register of the CPU and other things that you would not
ordinarily think about. But it can be very rewarding, both in
terms of performing useful tasks efficiently and in terms of
the understanding and insight you can gain into the machine
through writing a successful program.

     In this book, in addition to assuming that you have at
least a 16K Level II TRS-80 computer, we will also assume that
you have Radio Shack's Editor/Assembler program (catalog
number 26-2002), or an equivalent assembler such as Apparat's
EDTASM that comes with NEWDOS+. The Editor/Assembler program
will enable you to assemble programming code discussed in the
book by yourself. If you don't have an assembler, in many
cases you can still POKE program code into memory, or you
might even get by with a machine language monitor program
(such as my own Monitors #3 or #4). These allow you to enter
values into memory one byte at a time.   In any event, the
content of this book will become clear to you much faster if
you can try out the examples given by assembling them on your
own computer.

     To understand machine language, it is essential that you
understand the Z-80 microprocessor and the memory of the
TRS-80. The Z-80 is the microprocessor around which the
TRS-80 is built. Manufactured by Zilog, Inc., it is one of a
number of popular microprocessors including the 8080 and the

8008, both manufactured by Intel. The Z-80 does everything
that they do and more.

1.2 Basic Components of the Computer

Every computer consists of three basic components: the
CENTRAL PROCESSING UNIT, abbreviated CPU, which for the TRS-80
is the Z-80 microprocessor; a MEMORY, usually indicated as
some quantity of "K", where K equals 1024; and INPUT-OUTPUT
DEVICES, by which the computer communicates with the outside
world and vice-versa. You are no doubt familiar with most of
the input-output devices of the TRS-80, and if you don't have
all of them, you have surely seen them in Radio Shack
brochures or in stores. Everyone who has a TRS-80 has a video
monitor, keyboard, and cassette recorder. The video monitor
is an output device that actually displays a small portion of
memory. The keyboard, which you use to feed data into the
machine, is an input device. The cassette is used both for
input and for output. Other devices include floppy disk
drives, printers, and a variety of specialized equipment such
as the RS-232 interface and voice synthesizer.

1.3 The Memory of the TRS-80

The memory of the TRS-80 is contained in both the keyboard
case and the expansion interface. You are no doubt aware that
memory is not free, and so the amount of memory you have
depends on how much you have purchased. The basic unit of
memory in the TRS-80 is the BYTE, a number consisting of 8
bits or binary digits. A byte is capable of storing values
only between 0 and 255; all larger numbers must therefore be
contained in multiples of bytes. The largest value that can
be contained in a two-byte number is 65,535 and this number
is exactly the amount of memory that can be attached to the
Z-80 microprocessor. Each memory location is designated by a
two-byte number called its ADDRESS. Since the zero value is
used to indicate the first location, there are a total of
65,536 locations. In computer jargon, "K" indicates 1024 (2
to the tenth power) rather than 1000. Thus, the TRS-80 can
address a total of 64K bytes.

   There are three different kinds of memory used in the
TRS-80. First is the ROM or "read-only memory". Values can be
read out of ROM but not written into it, to prevent accidental
data destruction. ROM contains the Basic interpreter, which
is always there as soon as you power up the computer. When
you write a Basic program, it is actually data used by the ROM
program. The LOWER 12K bytes of memory are reserved for ROM.
0 to 4095 (4K) is used for Level I, and 0 to 12,287 (12K) is
used for Level II.

The second kind of memory used by the TRS-80 is RAM or
"random access memory". Numbers can be read or written in
RAM. RAM is used for your programs and data, but not all of
it is available to you. With a Level II computer, the first
822 locations are used by the system for a number of special
purposes that will be explained in detail in chapter 5. (With
Disk Basic, the first 10K of RAM is used!) The TRS-80 uses
only the upper 48K locations, 16,384 through 65,535, for RAM.
This is why the maximum RAM you can purchase is 48K. If you
have 4K RAM, it is located at 16,384 through 20,479; 16K runs
through 32,767, and 32K through 49,152.

That still leaves 4K. The area between 12,288 and 16,383
is used for MEMORY-MAPPED input-output devices. The upper 1K
(15,360 through 16,383) is used for the video display. What
you see on the video display is actually what' is stored in
this portion of memory. 14,336 through 14,464 is used for the
keyboard. The rest of this region is reserved for other
purposes, and only a few locations have actually been
implemented at this time.

The fact that the video display is memory-mapped means that
anything you put into these locations is immediately sent to
the display. You can try running the following Level II Basic
program to test this out:

```
10 INPUT A
20 CLS
30 FOR I=15360 TO 16383
40 POKE I,A
50 NEXT I
60 GOTO 10
```

"A" must be a value between 0 and 255 (the maximum value that
can be contained in a byte). Then look at Appendix C of the
LEVEL II BASIC REFERENCE MANUAL (Control, Graphics, and ASCII
codes). You will find that the number you input corresponds
to the code that is printed across the entire screen; but
when the program finishes, the question mark asking you to
input a new value is still at the upper left corner. Why?

The reason is that you have not issued a "PRINT" statement,
and have thus just bombed the video memory. Now you can see
that the PRINT statement in Basic actually does much more than
just print characters on the screen. It keeps track of where
the cursor is located, and when you come to the bottom of the
screen, it automatically scrolls everything up to the next
line, with the material at the top of the screen disappearing.
In addition, it responds to a number of special characters
called "control codes", which cause it to do such things as
home the cursor, clear the screen, clear to the end of the

line, backspace, and so forth. If you had to work all this
out every time you printed something, it would be a mess, and
in this case you would also be duplicating a feature already
implemented in the TRS-80's ROM. But now that you understand
that this is all there is to it, you may not be afraid of
working out your own display routine, if you have a reason to
do things differently from the way they are handled in the
ROM.

        1.4 Binary and Hexadecimal Numbers

The basic unit of TRS-80's memory is the byte. The value
contained in a specific byte, or the address where the byte is
located, can be denoted in three different ways: as a
DECIMAL, BINARY, or HEXADECIMAL number. We are most familiar
with the decimal or base 10 number system, and that is the
code that Radio Shack has used in the LEVEL II BASIC REFERENCE
MANUAL.   There is one important difference between the use of
these numbers in Basic and our ordinary use of them: in
Basic, the comma is used as a separator. Thus, if we write
"16,383" in a Basic program, it would actually indicate two
numbers, 16 and 383. To indicate this quantity as one number,
we must write "16383".   To avoid this confusion, we will
henceforth always write out five-digit or longer decimal
numbers without commas.

    In   a decimal number, each digit represents a value
multiplied by a power of 10.   For example, the number 934
equals 9 times 100 plus 3 times 10 plus 4 times 1. In other
number systems, the same relationship exists, except the
digits represent powers of the base number. The digits of
binary numbers represent powers of 2. In the binary number
system, each binary digit or "bit" can indicate only a value
of 0 or 1. Binary numbers require a great many digits to be
written out.   For example, 100000 binary equals 32 decimal.
Binary numbers are nevertheless important because   they
indicate the way numbers are actually represented inside the
computer.

    Because of the length of binary numbers, programmers have
adopted the hexadecimal or base 16 number system. Since 16 is
a power of 2 (the fourth), there is a direct relationship
between binary and hexadecimal numbers: each hexadecimal
digit indicates a 4-bit quantity. The value contained in any
byte can be expressed in exactly two hexadecimal digits.   In
the hexadecimal system, each digit can express a value between
0 and 15. The numerals 0 - 9 are used for those values, while
the letters A - F are used for 10 - 15. It may be awkward to
think of something like "FE" as a number, but it is much

easier to convert this number into binary form than the
equivalent decimal number 254.

To clarify the confusion resulting from the use of
different number systems, a letter or subscript is sometimes
appended to the number to indicate the number system. "B"
indicates binary and "H" hexadecimal, and the absence of any
letter indicates decimal. For example, both 100000B and 20H
indicate 32. In this book, the H subscript will normally be
appended to hexadecimal numbers unless it is supremely clear
from the context that the discussion involves only hexadecimal
numbers. This is a helpful convention because it is also used
by the TRS-80 Editor/Assembler.

(Programmers also sometimes employ another number system,
the octal or base 8 system. It is similar to hexadecimal in
that 8 is a power of 2 and each digit expresses a 3-bit
quantity, and in some cases easier to recognize because only
the numerals 0 - 7 are used. Octal is not used often with
byte-addressing computers, and we will not use it in this
book.)

1.5   ASCII

Everything inside the computer is indicated as a number. It
is what the number represents that determines the difference
between one thing and another. Numbers may represent
instructions to the computer to perform specific actions (a
program), values used in calculations (data), or characters to
be printed (ASCII code).

ASCII stands for "American Standard Code for Information
Interchange". Formulated many years ago and now implemented
in billions of dollars' worth of electronic equipment, it is
the method by which all of the characters are represented
numerically, whether entered from the keyboard or printed on
the video display. Although ASCII is only a 7-bit code, 8-bit
bytes are always used to hold the ASCII values within the
TRS-80. Appendix C of the LEVEL II BASIC REFERENCE MANUAL
lists the correspondences between the characters displayed and
the numerical values. For example, 32 indicates a blank
space, and 65 is the letter capital-A. Although the TRS-80
can display only upper-case letters on its video monitor, it
can input lower-case letters from the keyboard and hold them
in memory. Lower-case letters are produced by holding down
the shift key as you type a letter -- the reverse of a
typewriter keyboard -- but you cannot know that they are
lower-case letters because they are displayed as upper-case
letters. Furthermore, if you type in a Basic program in lower
case, it will be converted to upper case (although data values

used by Basic programs are not converted). The only
discrepancy is with the "@" key. "PRINT @" used with a "shift
@" will not work.

The important point about upper and lower case is that the
TRS-80 is fully capable of COMPUTING with lower-case letters;
it merely can't DISPLAY them. As this is being written,
several companies are offering lower-case modifications, and
Radio Shack itself has just released its own lower-case
modification which unfortunately is incompatible with both the
other methods and software written for them.

The 7-bit ASCII code has room for 128 values, but not all
of these are used for displayable characters. The first 32
values (0-31) are used for control codes, not all of which are
implemented on the TRS-80. Since the 7-bit values are always
kept in 8-bit bytes, that leaves room for 128 more values for
other purposes, and these values (128-255) are used for space-
compression codes, tab codes, and graphics.

1.6 Number Formats in Basic

Although numerical values used in computer calculations appear
to be the most straightforward kind of data, they are somewhat
more complicated because most values require several bytes.
Level II Basic has three kinds of numerical variables:
integers, single-, and double-precision floating-point
numbers. The simplest numbers are integers, which are held in
two bytes or 16 bits. Because the first bit is used for the
sign (plus is zero and minus is one), the maximum value of an
integer is 32767. There is one funny thing about 2-byte
integers, which is also true of all 2-byte values in the Z-80:
the two bytes are stored "backwards" in memory -- that is, the
least-significant byte is stored first, and the
most-significant byte last. To figure out what value is
represented, the order must be reversed. The reason for this
is simply that bytes were stored in this manner in the 8008
and 8080, and the Z-80 maintains compatibility with these
microprocessors.

Single- and double-precision floating-point numbers are
kept in groups of four and eight bytes, respectively. The
whole manner in which these calculations are carried out
inside the computer is very complicated, and will not be
discussed in detail in this book. We will nevertheless
explain more about them in chapters 10 and 11.

1.7 Analyzing Memory

Since everything inside the TRS-80, or any computer, is stored
in the form of 8-bit bytes, there is no way that you can know
whether they represent a program, data, or ASCII code, without
making an analysis, and this can be very complicated. To help
with making such an analysis, there are programs you can
purchase such as machine-language monitors or disassemblers.
A disassembler is the reverse of an assembler: instead of
assembling   symbolic   instructions into machine code, it
"disassembles" machine code into   symbolic   instructions.
Machine language monitors also provide commands for displaying
the memory in ASCII form or as hexadecimal numbers.

   The first part of this book will be devoted to explaining
the technical details about how the Z-80 microprocessor works
and other necessary facts about the TRS-80. The second part
will then be devoted to explaining practical problems that
involve everyday applications for TRS-80 machine language
programs.

2

THE ARCHITECTURE
OF THE Z-80 CPU

2.1 Registers

The Z-80 contains two sets of eight internal general-purpose registers, four 16-bit registers, and two special-purpose 8-bit registers. A REGISTER is a memory location within the CPU where computation may be carried out. One of the two sets of eight general-purpose registers is called the MAIN REGISTER SET and the other is called the ALTERNATE REGISTER SET. The main set is what you always use in computations. The alternate set is accessed by only two instructions which exchange the contents of the main set with the alternate set. The general-purpose registers are called by the names A, F, B, C, D, E, H, and L. A is also called the ACCUMULATOR, and it is the most important register in the computer, because it is where most of the action takes place. F is also called the FLAG register or FLAGS, because it is where bits indicating various conditions are kept. F itself is never used in computations. It is automatically set according to the RESULTS of other computations. The remaining registers B through L may be used either as 8-bit registers or in PAIRS for 16-bit quantities. In the latter case, B and C, D and E, and H and L are always used together, and, in such cases, are designated as BC, DE, and HL. Figure 2-1 shows a diagram of the registers in the Z-80 CPU.

MAIN REG SET		ALTERNATE REG SET		
ACCUMULATOR A	FLAGS F	ACCUMULATOR A'	FLAGS F'	
B	C	B'	C'	GENERAL PURPOSE REGISTERS
D	E	D'	E'	
H	L	H'	L'	

INTERRUPT VECTOR I	MEMORY REFRESH R	SPECIAL PURPOSE REGISTERS
INDEX REGISTER IX		
INDEX REGISTER IY		
STACK POINTER SP		
PROGRAM COUNTER PC		

Figure 1: The registers in the Z-80 CPU

Two of the 16-bit registers are called INDEX REGISTERS, designated IX and IY. They are used, more or less, as pointers to a memory location to which an offset value can be added or subtracted. The other two 16-bit registers are called the STACK POINTER and the PROGRAM COUNTER. The program counter, abbreviated PC, determines the order in which instructions are executed. When an instruction is being executed, the PC contains the address of the NEXT instruction to be executed. A branch or jump instruction actually modifies the PC. The stack pointer, SP, contains an address that must point to a free area in RAM that is used for temporary storage of values as the computer is running. If the stack ever gets destroyed, or if it points to an area in ROM or nonexistent memory, disaster can occur! The use of the stack pointer will be discussed in detail in chapter 4.

The remaining 8-bit registers are called the interrupt (I) and refresh (R) registers. The refresh register makes it easy and practical to use low-cost dynamic RAM rather than static RAM in the computer. The latter RAM also produces significantly greater heat. (The TRS-80 uses dynamic RAM.) Otherwise, the refresh register is unimportant from the

programmer's standpoint.   The interrupt register provides a
more flexible system of interrupts for the Z-80 than the 8080.
Interrupts, however, are used only for more advanced real-time
programming and are beyond the scope of this book.

Perhaps you are wondering about the differences between the
Z-80 and the 8080 microprocessors.   The 8080 has the same
8-bit general registers as the Z-80, but no alternate register
set.   In addition, it has no index registers (IX or   IY)   nor
the interrupt or refresh registers. The instruction set of
the Z-80 will, therefore, be much larger than that of the
8080, because it includes all of the instructions involving
these registers.   There are very few of the remaining
instructions, however, that the 8080 does not also execute.

In general, it is the programmer's responsibility to keep
track of all the registers he is using and whether their
contents can be changed without causing the program to produce
an error.   The contents of any register pair can easily be
saved and retrieved, by being pushed onto or popped off the
stack.   This method can be used to free a register pair for
use in a series of calculations without losing its value. One
of the things that beginners often complain about with
assembly-language programming is that it seems difficult
because there are so many registers to keep track of.
Actually, having many registers is an asset, and programming
the computer is easier than it would be if there were fewer of
them to look after! But there is nothing that you as a
programmer can do to change the structure of the CPU, so the
only thing to do is to learn how it works and take advantage
of its inherent properties.

2.2 Instruction Mnemonics and Operands

In describing the instructions executed by nearly all
computers, the term LOAD is used to indicate a transfer of
data between a memory location and a register in the CPU.
STORE indicates the opposite transfer, from a register to
memory, and MOVE indicates a transfer of data from within the
instruction itself (IMMEDIATE data) to a register. When Zilog
designed the Z-80, they decided to scrap some of this
terminology. All instructions that specify a transfer of data
between a register and a memory location on the Z-80 are
called LOAD instructions, abbreviated by the mnemonic LD. The
direction of the transfer is indicated by the ORDER of the
operands.

If register A is loaded from location 100, this would be
specified by the mnemonic:

```
        LD    A,(100)
```

whereas if location 100 were loaded from register A, it would
be:

```
        LD    (100),A
```

The parentheses around 100 are necessary to show that 100 is
the ADDRESS of the memory location involved in the transfer.
Lack of parentheses would indicate a move instruction:

```
        LD    A,100
```

means that A is loaded with the VALUE 100. (The fourth
possibility in this progression, "LD   100,A" would be
meaningless. It would indicate that the value 100 were loaded
from A, but doing so might change "100" to some other value!)

    It is very important that you understand the meaning of the
parentheses in these instructions, as this terminology is
basic to descriptions of all instructions on the Z-80.
Whenever parentheses enclose an operand in a Zilog mnemonic,
it means that the operand specifies an address rather than a
data value. An unparenthesized "HL" specifies the HL register
pair, whereas "(HL)" indicates that the CONTENTS of HL specify
an address which is involved in a data transfer.

    What is particularly confusing about this terminology is
that the Z-80 was designed as an upgrading of the 8080
microprocessor, so that it was 100 per cent compatible for
executing 8080 instructions. Any 8080 program will run on the
Z-80, and the Z-80 will do much more besides. But in order
for people to transfer their programs to the Z-80, a whole new
terminology had to be learned. This upset some people so much
that they invented their own terminology, designed as
extensions of the 8080's, and implemented it in assembler
programs and documentation. Nowadays, however, most people
use Zilog's terminology, recognizing that it is different from
Intel's. (It has been rumored that Zilog had to invent a new
set of mnemonics for legal reasons, because Intel had
copyrighted its own.) For our purposes, one set of mnemonics
is enough to learn, and the fact that Radio Shack has used
Zilog's terminology throughout its documentation and the
Editor/Assembler program more than tips the balance in that
direction.

                    2.3 Uses of the Registers

The registers of the Z-80 CPU must always be considered in
relation to the operations that can be carried out in them.

While there are many operations that can only be done in
certain registers, there are many others that can be carried
out in any register. A, the accumulator, is the most
important register. All 8-bit arithmetic and logical
operations involve the accumulator containing one of the
operands and the result of the operation. In addition, some
instructions that fetch or store a byte in memory only allow A
to be used; getting the byte into or out of another register
requires an additional operation. The flag register F is the
other "half" of the A register. By having F grouped with A in
the CPU, all registers can be treated in two-byte groups.

The HL register pair has two primary uses. First, it is
the "accumulator" for 16-bit arithmetic operations. (There
are no 16-bit logical operations.) All 16-bit arithmetic
operations use HL as one of the operand registers and the
result register. Second, HL can be used to contain an address
pointing to a memory location whose contents are used in an
8-bit operation. Whenever this is done, the operand is
indicated as "(HL)". While the BC and DE register pairs can
sometimes be used in this manner, there are many more Z-80
instructions that involve (HL). (In 8080 mnemonics, (HL) is
specified as M, meaning "memory".)

Both the individual register B and the BC register pair are
often used to hold a COUNT of the number of times something is
to be repeated, so these are sometimes called the "count"
registers. B is used as a count with the DJNZ instruction,
the mnemonic for which is supposed to suggest the mellifluous
phrase "decrement B and branch to the location specified if it
is not zero". The BC register pair is used as a count for all
block transfer instructions -- LDI, LDIR, etc. These
operations are used to move an entire block of memory from one
area to another, and they will be described in chapter 3.
Finally, the C register is the only register used for certain
input and output operations.

The DE register pair has many uses analogous to HL and BC,
except that there are fewer such instructions. Both (BC) and
(DE) can be used to specify addresses like (HL), but only
loading to or from the accumulator is possible. Thus,

                    LD   A,(DE)
and
                    LD   (BC),A

are legal, but not

                    LD   H,(BC)

whereas

NOT TO ACCUM
" FRom "

                    LD   H,(HL)

is legal.

                        2.4   Flags

The flag register F is never used to hold data. It contains
several bits logically called "flags", that are set according
to the RESULTS of other calculations. It is an eight-bit
register, even though there are only six flags, and only four
of   these   are   really   important   for most programming
applications. These four flags are called the ZERO flag (Z),
the SIGN flag (S), the CARRY flag (C), and the PARITY/OVERFLOW
flag (P/V). The other two flags, the HALF-CARRY flag (H)   and
the ADD/SUBTRACT flag (N), are used only with the DAA (decimal
adjust accumulator) instruction, which is used only for BCD
numbers, a relatively rare application.

     The carry flag C (not to be confused with register C!) is
set whenever an add instruction produces a result that is one
bit too large to be contained in a single register.
Correspondingly, it is also set when a subtract operation
produces a borrow. Since the Z-80 performs only addition and
subtraction of 8-bit and 16-bit values, the carry flag is
necessary not only for addition and subtraction of larger
values, but also for implementing software routines for
multiplication and division.   These operations will   be
discussed in chapter 13. The carry flag is also affected by
shift and rotate instructions, and it is cleared (set to zero)
by logical operations. "No carry" is indicated "NC".

     The zero flag is set only if the result of an operation is
zero.   "Non zero" is indicated "NZ". The sign flag, which is
indicated by the conditions plus (P) or minus (M), is a copy
of the sign bit (7) of the accumulator. The zero, sign, and
carry flags can also be set by compare instructions. The P/V
flag, indicated by the conditions PE (parity even) or PO
(parity odd), is used both for overflow conditions and to
indicate parity, depending on the instruction. Overflow means
that the result of an operation produced a value too large to
be contained in the register, whereas parity means that the
sum of the bits in the register is odd (PO) or even (PE). The
flag is also used for other purposes, such as during the
execution of block transfer instructions.

     Except for arithmetic, shift, and rotate instructions that
use the carry flag, the flags are USED only by the jump, call,
and   return   instructions.   (They   are SET by other
instructions.) These are CONDITIONAL operations that are
executed only if the condition they specify is true.

2.5 Addressing Modes

Addressing modes summarize all the ways in which instructions may be executed on the computer. To perform any operation involving memory, the computer must know the address of the location involved. For convenience of programming, there are always many ways in which addresses may be specified. The ZILOG Z80-CPU TECHNICAL MANUAL gives ten addressing modes for the Z-80. They can be described as follows:

(1) IMMEDIATE: A byte contained in the instruction is moved to a register.
     Instruction length = 2 bytes.
     Example: LD   A,1
     A is loaded with the value 1.

(2) IMMEDIATE EXTENDED: Same as above, except a two-byte value is moved to a register pair.
     Length = 3 bytes.
     Example: LD   HL,1000
     The HL register pair is loaded with the value 1000.

(3) RELATIVE: Applies only to the jump relative (JR) instructions. The value in the following byte is added to the location contained in the PC to determine the next address. The address indicated must lie in the range -128 to +127 bytes from the present instruction.
     Length = 2 bytes.
     Example: JR $+10
     ("$" means "address of the current instruction".) Jumps to the location 10 bytes following the present one.

(4) EXTENDED: The address of the operand is specified in the instruction.
     Length = 3 or 4 bytes.
     Example: LD   A,(1000)
     A is loaded from location 1000.

(5) INDEXED: The address of an operand is determined by adding a byte called a DISPLACEMENT to the value contained in an index register.
     Length = 3 or 4 bytes.
     Example: LD   A,(IX+5)
     A is loaded from the location whose address is computed by adding 5 to the value in index register IX.

(6) REGISTER: One register is loaded from another one.
     Length = 1 byte.
     Example: LD   B,C
     B is loaded from C.

(7)   IMPLIED: Not really a different mode! This means that a
       register is not indicated in the mnemonic, but
       implied by it.
       Length: 1 or 2 bytes.
       Example: SUB   B
       B is subtracted (from A, by implication).

(8)   REGISTER INDIRECT: The address of an operand is
       contained in a register pair (BC, DE, or HL).
       Length = 1 byte.
       Example: LD   A,(BC)
       A is loaded from the location whose address is contained
       in the BC register pair.

(9)   BIT: An individual bit in a register is set, reset, or
       tested.
       Length = 2 bytes.
       Example: SET   6,B
       Bit 6 in register B is set to 1.

(1Ø)   MODIFIED PAGE ZERO: Applies only to the restart (RST)
       instructions.   Only three BITS of the address are
       specified in the instruction itself.   The address must
       be a multiple of 8 between Ø and 56.
       Length = 1 byte.
       Example: RST   8
       A call is made to location 8.

                    2.6   Instruction Timing

All microcomputers are run by means of a CLOCK which provides
a basic frequency according to that instructions are executed.
While the clock frequency of the Z-8Ø can be as high as 4 MHz
(millions of cycles per second), the TRS-8Ø uses a clock
frequency of approximately 1.77 MHz, corresponding to a period
of 563 nanoseconds (billionths of a second). The Z-8Ø CPU
executes its instructions by going through a combination of a
few basic operations. They include memory read or write, I/O
device read or write, and interrupt acknowledge operations.
Each of these may require from three to six clock periods,
which are referred to as T cycles.   The basic operations
themselves are referred to as M (machine) cycles.

    The TRS-8Ø EDITOR ASSEMBLER USER INSTRUCTION MANUAL
discusses   each   instruction   of   the Z-8Ø separately, and
provides information on the number of M and T cycles required.
It also provides a figure of "4 MHZ E.T.", meaning 4 MHz
execution time. This is misleading, because the TRS-8Ø does
not run at 4 MHz (although the TRS-8Ø Model II does).
Instruction execution times in the manual must be multiplied

by approximately 2.26 in order to determine the actual TRS-80 time. The manual shows execution times ranging from 1.0 to 5.75 microseconds (millionths of a second), thus corresponding to 2.26 to 13 microseconds for the TRS-80. The fact that the TRS-80 can execute over 440,000 operations in one second is a true measure of its amazing computing power.

3

OVERVIEW OF THE Z-80 INSTRUCTION SET

Once you are familiar with the registers and internal
architecture of the Z-80 CPU, the next thing you probably are
wondering about is the operations that the computer can
execute. Our intention in this chapter is merely to give a
summary of the instructions that the Z-80 can execute -- not
to describe their operation in full. Complete tables of the
Z-80 instructions are given in Appendix A. Since the really
important point about assembly language programming is being
able to write programs that DO something, it is better to
study the function of individual instructions in the context
of programming examples. The second part of this book is
devoted to practical applications of TRS-80 assembly language
programming.

An operation executed by the computer may affect or be
affected by three different types of items, which are
specified as OPERANDS. Most operations involve the use of one
or more REGISTERS. These include either the main register set
(A, B, C, D, E, H, and L) and the index registers (IX and IY),
which are the ones you normally think about, or the stack
pointer (SP) and program counter (PC), which you may not think
of as holding data as the others do. The Z-80 often treats
the operand (HL), which refers to the memory location pointed
to by the H and L register pair, as a single register
analogous to one of the main registers, even though operations
referring to (HL) are always listed as "separate" operations
in the tables. The alternate register set is used by only two

18

instructions --   EXX and EX AF,AF' -- which exchange their
contents with the main register set.   Any   subsequent
computations are carried out using the main registers only.

   The next type of operand might include one or more MEMORY
LOCATIONS in the computer.   A few instructions can affect
entire blocks of data, but most affect only one or two bytes.

   The third type of operand includes the CONDITION CODES.
Sometimes a condition code is indicated in the instruction
itself, such as a jump on non-zero. At other times, one or
more condition codes are set according to the results of
computations carried out. It is the latter situation that is
indicated in the instruction tables, since the instructions
that use the condition codes do not alter them.

   Other information you might want to know about   Z-8Ø
instructions includes how many bytes they occupy, how long
they take to execute (in M or T cycles), and their object
codes.   We will refer to instruction times only by T cycles,
which are 563 nanoseconds for the TRS-8Ø (25Ø nanoseconds for
the TRS-8Ø model II).   This value must be multiplied by the
number of T cycles to determine the actual instruction time.

   Many people get confused by the concept of object code,
thinking that there is some mysterious force inside the
computer that causes it to run.   Actually, it is just a
succession of numbers stored in memory.   Since a byte can
contain 256 different values, you might think that there would
be 256 Z-8Ø instructions. In fact, there are many more than
this   number   because,   the   Z-8Ø has several different
instruction formats requiring from one to four bytes.   How
many instruction there are depends on how you count. For
example, "LD r,r'" which copies the contents of one register
into another, is listed as one instruction; but when you
consider that there are seven different registers that may
occupy either position in the instruction, then there are 49
instructions included under this one mnemonic. When you count
instructions in this way, there are 666 of them for the Z-8Ø.

   In Zilog's terminology, the ORDER of the operands indicates
the   function   of   the   items   involved in data transfer
instructions. The first operand is the DESTINATION operand
and the second is the SOURCE. For example, "LD A,B" indicates
that B is copied into A, whereas "LD B,A" indicates that A is
copied into B.

   If an operand is enclosed in parentheses, it means that the
operand refers to the CONTENTS of a register or memory
location. Unparenthesized operands denote either IMMEDIATE
DATA or the ADDRESS of a memory location.

Z-80 instructions have been divided into eleven groups by the manufacturer ZILOG. Most books use this grouping as the point of departure for discussing the instructions, and we will do the same here. In our listings below, the following abbreviations will be used:

r	single register: A, B, C, D, E, H or L.
IR	index register: IX or IY.
(IR+d)	the contents of an address determined by adding a displacement byte (d) to an index register.
s	a single register operand, which may be any of the following: r, n, (HL), or (IR+d).
dd	double register: BC, DE, HL, or SP.
qq	double register: BC, DE, HL, or AF.
pp	double register: BC, DE, SP, and either IX or IY depending on the operation.
n	a single byte contained within the instruction itself.
(n)	in input and output instructions, a byte contained within the instruction, whose value selects an I/O port.
nn	two data bytes contained within the instruction itself.
(nn)	a two-byte value contained within the instruction, referring to a memory address.
e	in jump relative instructions, a value added to the current value of the PC to determine a branch address.
p	in RST (restart) instructions, address of the location called: a multiple of 8 between 0 and 56.
b	bit: 0, 1, 2, 3, 4, 5, 6, or 7.
cc	condition code: NZ, Z, NC, C, PO, PE, P, M.
c	condition code in jump relative instruction: NZ, Z, NC, or C.
(HL)	the contents of the memory location pointed by the HL register pair. Similar use is made of (BC) and (DE).
I or R	the Interrupt or refresh registers.
<=	This symbol is used to indicate that the operand on the right is copied to the operand on the left.
=>	This symbol is used in right shift and rotate instructions, to indicate that the operand on the left is copied to the operand on the right.
<=>	This symbol indicates that the two operands are exchanged or swapped.
8080	When indicated in a note field, this means that the instruction also exists on the 8080 microprocessor.

3.1 Eight-Bit Load Group

All the instructions in this group transfer (copy) one byte of
data between two CPU registers, or between a CPU register and
a single memory location. Confusingly, Zilog refers to all
such   instructions   as   "loading",   whereas   most computer
manufacturers have used "load" only to refer to a transfer
from memory to a register. Moving data from a register to
memory is called "storing".

   Since none of these operands except LD A,I and LD A,R
affect the condition codes, they are not mentioned in the
table below.

Instruction	Length (Bytes)	No. of T Cycles	Notes	Function
LD r,r'	1	4	8080	r <= r'
LD r,n	2	7	8080	r <= n
LD r,(HL)	1	7	8080	r <= (HL)
LD r,(IR+d)	3	19		r <= (IR+d)
LD (HL),r	1	7	8080	(HL) <= r
LD (IR+d),r	3	19		(IR+d) <= r
LD (HL),n	2	10	8080	(HL) <= r
LD A,(BC)	1	7	8080	A <= (BC)
LD A,(DE)	1	7	8080	A <= (DE)
LD A,(nn)	3	13	8080	A <= (nn)
LD (BC),A	1	7	8080	(BC) <= A
LD (DE),A	1	7	8080	(DE) <= A
LD (nn),A	3	13	8080	(nn) <= A
LD A,I	2	9	1	A <= I register
LD A,R	2	9	1	A <= R register
LD I,A	2	9		I register <= A
LD R,A	2	9		R register <= A

Notes:

(1) Z and S flags set according to the results of the
instruction.   The interrupt enable flip/flop is copied to the
P/V flag.

3.2 Sixteen-Bit Load Group

These instructions are similar to the eight-bit loads, except
that sixteen bits of data are involved in the transfer. No
condition codes are affected by these instructions.

Instruction	Length (Bytes)	No. of T Cycles	Notes	Function
LD dd,nn	3	10	8080	dd <= nn
LD IR,nn	4	14		IR <= nn
LD HL,(nn)	3	16	8080	HL <= (nn)
LD dd,(nn)	4	20		dd <= (nn)
LD IR,(nn)	4	20		IR <= (nn)
LD (nn),HL	3	16	8080	(nn) <= HL
LD (nn),dd	4	20		(nn) <= dd
LD (nn),IR	4	20		(nn) <= IR
LD SP,HL	1	6	8080	SP <= HL
LD SP,IR	2	10		SP <= IR
PUSH qq	1	11	8080	(SP-2) <= qq(L) (SP-1) <= qq(H) SP <= SP-2
PUSH IR	2	15		(SP-2) <= IR(L) (SP-1) <= IR(H) SP <= SP-2
POP qq	1	10	8080	qq(H) <= (SP+1) qq(L) <= (SP) SP <= SP+2
POP IR	2	14		IR(H) <= (SP+1) IR(L) <= (SP) SP <= SP+2

3.3 Exchange and Block Transfer and Search Group

These instructions really include two different groups:
exchange instructions, which swap two sets of operands, a~d
block transfer and search instructions, which move or compare
large blocks of data. These will be described in more detail
in later chapters, but a summary of their operations is
presented here.

Instruction	Length (Bytes)	No. of T Cycles	Notes	Function
EX DE,HL	1	4	8080	DE <=> HL
EX AF,AF'	1	4		AF <=> AF'
EXX	1	4		BC <=> BC' DE <=> DE' HL <=> HL'
EX (SP),HL	1	19	8080	H <=> (SP+1) L <=> (SP)
EX (SP),IR	2	23		IR(1) <=> (SP+1) IR(2) <=> (SP)
LDI	2	16	1	(DE) <= (HL) DE <= DE+1 HL <= HL+1 BC <= BC-1

Instruction	(Bytes)	Cycles	Notes	Function
LDIR	2	21 if BC<>0 16 if BC=0	2	(DE) <= (HL) DE <= DE+1 HL <= HL+1 BC <= BC-1 Repeat till BC=0
LDD	2	16	1	(DE) <= (HL) DE <= DE-1 HL <= HL-1 BC <= BC-1
LDDR	2	21 if BC<>0 16 if BC=0	2	(DE) <= (HL) DE <= DE-1 HL <= HL-1 BC <= BC-1 Repeat till BC=0
CPI	2	16	3	A compared to (HL) HL <= HL+1 BC <= BC-1
CPIR	2	21 if BC<>0 and A<>(HL) 16 if BC=0 or A=(HL)	3	A compared to (HL) HL <= HL+1 BC <= BC-1 Repeat till A=(HL) or BC=0
CPD	2	16	3	A compared to (HL) HL <= HL-1 BC <= BC-1
CPDR	2	21 if BC<>0 and A<>(HL) 16 if BC=0 or A=(HL)	3	A compared to (HL) HL <= HL-1 BC <= BC-1 Repeat till A=(HL) or BC=0

Notes:
(1) P/V flag set according to result of operation.
     N and H set to zero.

(2) P/V flag set to 0 at conclusion of operation.
     N and H set to zero.

(3) P/V flag = 0 if result of BC-1=0, otherwise P/V=1.
     Z flag is 1 if A=(HL), otherwise 0.   N set to 1.
     S and H flag set according to result of compare.

        3.4 Eight-Bit Arithmetic and Logical Group

These instructions perform arithmetic and logical operations
on single-byte quantities.   Except for the increment and
decrement instructions, all arithmetic is carried out only in
the accumulator, although the operand A is not indicated in

some of the instruction mnemonics. Condition codes are set by
every one of the operations, as explained in the notes. The
symbol "CY" indicates the carry bit or C flag, which is used
in certain arithmetic operations. The full range of
instruction operands is shown only for the ADD instruction.
The number of T cycles and condition codes for individual
instructions of the other operations is the same as for the
corresponding instruction shown for ADD. The logical
operations AND, OR, and XOR are indicated by the words since
the symbols do nt exist on the TRS-80's keyboard.

Instruction	Length (Bytes)	No. of T Cycles	Notes	Function
ADD A,r	1	4	8080,1	A <= A + r
ADD A,n	2	7	8080,1	A <= A + n
ADD A,(HL)	1	7	8080,1	A <= A + (HL)
ADD A,(IR+d)	3	19	1	A <= A + (IR+d)
ADC A,s	1-3	4-19	8080,1	A <= A + s + CY
SUB s	1-3	4-19	8080,2	A <= A - s
SBC A,s	1-3	4-19	8080,2	A <= A - s - CY
AND s	1-3	4-19	8080,3	A <= A AND s
OR s	1-3	4-19	8080,3	A <= A OR s
XOR s	1-3	4-19	8080,3	A <= A XOR s
CP s	1-3	4-19	8080,6	A - s
INC r	1	4	8080,4	r <= r + 1
INC (HL)	1	11	8080,4	(HL) <= (HL) + 1
INC (IR+d)	3	23	4	(IR+d) <= (IR+d)+1
DEC r	1	4	8080,5	r <= r -1
DEC (HL)	1	11	8080,5	(HL) <= (HL) - 1
DEC (IR+d)	3	23	5	(IR+d) <= (IR+d)-1

Notes:
(1) C, S, Z, and H set according to the result of the
operation. The P/V flag contains the overflow of the result
of the operation. N set to 0.

(2) Condition codes set as in note 1, except N set to 1. IR
instructions do not exist on the 8080.

(3) S, Z, and H set according to the result of the operation.
C and N set to zero. The P/V flag is set if the resulting
parity is even, otherwise reset.

(4) All codes set as in note 1, except C unaffected.

(5) All codes set as in note 2, except C unaffected.

(6) Compare operations perform a subtract but leave the
operands unaffected, thus changing only the condition codes,
which are set as in note 2.

3.5 General-Purpose Arithmetic and CPU Control Groups

This group includes a bunch of miscellaneous instructions. The operation of the DAA instruction is too complicated to describe here, but will be explained in more detail below.

Instruction	Length (Bytes)	No. of T Cycles	Notes	Function
DAA	1	4	8080,1	Decimal adjust accumulator
CPL	1	4	8080,2	Complement: accumulator (one's complement: zeros changed to ones, ones to zeros.
NEG	2	4	3	Negate accumulator (two's complement)
CCF	1	4	8080,4	Complement carry flag
SCF	1	4	8080,5	Set carry flag
NOP	1	4	8080,6	No operation
HALT	1	4	8080,6	CPU operation suspended
DI	1	4	8080,6	Disable Interrupts
EI	1	4	8080,6	Enable Interrupts
IM 0	2	8	6	Interrupt mode 0
IM 1	2	8	6	Interrupt mode 1
IM 2	2	8	6	Interrupt mode 2

Notes:

(1) C, Z, S, P/V, and H flags set according to result of operation. P/V indicates parity. N unaffected.

(2) C, Z, S, and P/V flags unaffected. N and H set to 1.

(3) C, Z, S, P/V, and H flags set according to result of operation. P/V indicates overflow. N set to 1.

(4) C set according to operation. Z, P/V, and S unaffected. H unknown, N set to 1.

(5) C set to 1, N and H to 0. Z, P/V, and S unaffected.

(6) No flags affected.

3.6 16-Bit Arithmetic Group

These operations perform arithmetic calculations on 16-bit quantities. For most of the operations, the HL register pair is used as an "accumulator" just as the A register is used for the 8-bit operations. This means that HL is used to hold one of the operands, and it contains the result after the operation is executed. The index registers can also be used in this way for additions.

Instruction	Length (Bytes)	No. of T Cycles	Notes	Function
ADD HL,ss	1	11	8080,1	HL <= HL + ss
ADC HL,ss	2	15	2	HL <= HL + ss + CY
SBC HL,ss	2	15	2	HL <= HL - ss - CY
ADD IR,pp	2	15	1	IR <= IR + pp
INC ss	1	6	8080,3	ss <= ss + 1
INC IR	2	10	3	IR <= IR + 1
DEC ss	1	6	8080,3	ss <= ss - 1
DEC IR	2	10	3	IR <= IR - 1

Notes:
(1) C set according to the result of the operation.   S, Z, and P/V unaffected. N set to 0, H unknown.

(2) C, S, Z, and P/V set according to the result of the operation. P/V indicates overflow. N set to 0 for ADC, 1 for SBC. H unknown.

(3) No flags affected. (N.B.)

3.7 Rotate and Shift Group

These instructions include a large number of operations that shift or rotate single registers. There are several redundancies among them, because the Z-80 executes both the 8080 instructions, which use only the accumulator, and unique Z-80 instructions, which use every possible register. All shifts or rotates move the affected register by only one bit.

    A SHIFT operation moves each bit in a register to the next bit, in a left or right direction, and fills in the vacated bit with a zero. A ROTATE operation, of which there are far more than shifts, moves the bit shifted off the end around to the other side. All of this gets complicated by the way in which the carry bit participates in the operation. There are both 8-bit instructions, in which a bit is moved both into or out of the carry bit and into the register, and 9-bit instructions, in which the carry bit participates as if it

were an extra bit in the register. The N and H flags are
reset by all of these instructions, and the P/V flag indicates
parity. The operation of the RLD and RRD instructions, which
are intended for BCD operations, are too complicated to
describe here, but will be explained in more detail below.

Instruction		Length (Bytes)	No. of T Cycles	Notes	Function
RLCA		1	4	8080,1	Rotate A left circular CY & bit 0 <= bit 7
RLA		1	4	8080,1	Rotate left accumulator CY <= bit 7 a bit 0 <= CY
RRCA		1	4	8080,1	Rotate A right circular bit 0 => CY & bit 7
RRA		1	4	8080,1	Rotate right accumulator bit 0 => CY CY => bit 7
RLC	r	2	8	2	Rotate left circular r (Same as RLCA, but for any register)
RLC	(HL)	2	15	2	Rotate left circular (HL)
RLC	(IR+d)	2	23	2	Rotate left circular (IR+d)
RL	s	2	8-23	2	Rotate left s (Same as RLA, but for any r, (HL), or (IR+d))
RRC	s	2	8-23	2	Rotate right circular s (Same as RRCA but for any s)
RR	s	2	8-23	2	Rotate right s (Same as RRA but for any s)
SLA	s	2	8-23	2	Shift left arithmetic s CY <= bit 7 bit 0 <= 0
SRA	s	2	8-23	2	Shift right arithmetic s bit 0 => CY bit 7 unchanged
SRL	s	2	8-23	2	Shift right logical s bit 0 => CY 0 => bit 7
RLD		2	18	3	Rotate digit left
RRD		2	18	3	Rotate digit right

Notes:
(1) C set according to result of operation. S, Z, and P/V
unaffected.

(2) C, Z, S, and P/V set according to result of operation.

(3)   Z, S, and P/V set according to result of operation. C unaffected.

3.8 Bit Set, Reset, and Test Group

All of these operations exist only on the Z-80 -- none on the 8080. A BIT operation is a bit test for zero. SET sets a bit to 1; RESET sets it to 0.

Instruction	Length (Bytes)	No. of T Cycles	Notes	Function
BIT b,r	2	8	1	Bit b in register r tested
BIT b,(HL)	2	12	1	Bit b in location (HL) tested
BIT b,(IR+d)	4	20	1	Bit b in location (IR+d) tested
SET b,r	2	8	2	Bit b in register r set to 1
SET b,(HL)	2	15	2	Bit b in (HL) set
SET b,(IR+d)	4	23	2	Bit b in (IR+d) set
RES b,s	2-4	8-23	2	Bit b in s reset (s may be any r, (HL), or (IR+d))

Notes:
(1) Z set according to result of operation. C unaffected.
     S and P/V unknown. N set to 0, H to 1.

(2) No flags affected.

3.9 Jump Group

These instructions branch to a location specified, often depending on a particular condition. Sometimes the branch address is contained within the instruction. In the case of jump relative instructions, the branch address is determined by adding a displacement value e to the current contents of the program counter. None of these instructions affects the condition codes.

Instruction	Length (Bytes)	No. of T Cycles	Notes	Function
JP nn	3	10	8080	PC <= nn
JP cc,nn	3	10	8080	If cc true, PC <= nn
				Continue if cc false
JR e	2	12		PC <= PC + e
JR c,e	2	7		Continue if c false
		12		If c true,
				PC <= PC + e
JP (HL)	1	4	8080	PC <= (HL)
JP (IR)	2	8		PC <= (IR)
DJNZ e	2			B <= B - 1
		8		If B = 0, continue
		13		If B<>0, PC <= PC+e

3.10   Call and Return Group

Call instructions push the present contents of the PC onto the stack and branch to a specified location. Return instructions pop the contents off the top of the stack and branch to the resulting location, thus resuming execution from the instruction immediately following the call.   A restart instruction is identical to a call, except that the location called is specified in only three bits, and must lie within the first 64 bytes of memory.   None of these instructions affects the condition codes.

Instruction	Length (Bytes)	No. of T Cycles	Notes	Function
CALL nn	3	17	8080	(SP-1) <= PC(H)
				(SP-2) <= PC(L)
				PC <= nn
CALL cc,nn	3	10	8080	If cc false, continue
		17		If cc true,
				same as CALL
RET	1	10	8080	PC(L) <= (SP)
				PC(H) <= (SP+1)
RET cc	1	5	8080	If cc false, continue
		11		If cc true,
				same as RET
RETI	2	14		Return from interupt
				(same as RET)
RETN	2	14		Return from non-
				maskable interrupt
RST p	1	11	8080,1	(SP-1) <= PC(H)
				(SP-2) <= PC(L)
				PC(H) <= 0
				PC(L) <= p

Notes:
(1)   p must be a multiple of 8 from 0 to 56.

3.11   Input and Output Group

These instructions transfer a byte of data between a CPU register and an external input/output device, accessed through an I/O port specified in the instruction. The symbol (n) indicates that the value n specifies the port, whereas (C) indicates that the port number is taken from register C. Some of these instructions transfer entire blocks of data at a time. Except for the 8080-compatible instructions, the contents of register B are placed on the top half of the address bus. This is a negligible factor for the TRS-80.

Instruction	Length (Bytes)	No. of T Cycles	Notes	Function
IN A,(n)	2	11	8080,1	A <= (n)
IN r,(C)	2	12	2	r <= (C)
INI	2	16	3	(HL) <= (C)
				B <= B-1
				HL <= HL+1
INIR	2	21 if BC<>0	4	(HL) <= (C)
		16 if BC=0		B <= B-1
				HL <= HL+1
IND	2	16	3	(HL) <= (C)
				B <= B-1
				HL <= HL-1
INDR	2	21 if BC<>0	4	(HL) <= (C)
		16 if BC=0		B <= B-1
				HL <= HL-1
OUT (n),A	2	11	8080,1	(n) <= A
OUT (C),r	2	12	1	(C) <= r
OUTI	2	16	3	(C) <= (HL)
				B <= B-1
				HL <= HL+1
OTIR	2	21 if BC<>0	4	(C) <= (HL)
		16 if BC=0		B <= B-1
				HL <= HL+1
OUTD	2	16	3	(C) <= (HL)
				B <= B-1
				HL <= HL-1
OTDR	2	21 if BC<>0	4	(C) <= (HL)
		16 if BC=0		B <= B-1
				HL <= HL-1

Notes:
(1)   Condition codes unaffected.

(2) C unaffected. S, Z, P/V and H set according to result of operation. N set to Ø. P/V indicates parity.

(3) C unaffected, Z set according to result of operation.   N set to 1. P/V, S, and H unknown.

(4) C unaffected. Z and N set to 1. Other flags unknown.

4

THE STACK AND
ITS APPLICATIONS

4.1   The Stack Area and Stack Pointer

The STACK is an area in memory where data values from the CPU
registers can be stored and retrieved. The STACK POINTER (SP)
is a 16-bit register in the CPU that contains the address of
the current location that is at the "top" of the stack.   The
need for a stack area may seem strange, since data may always
be stored or retrieved by using the LD instructions.   Many
earlier computers did not have a stack area. Understanding
the use of the stack is crucial to writing any assembly
language program for the TRS-80, for if the stack or stack
pointer ever get destroyed, the entire computer will not run!

    The idea of having a general area in memory for storing and
retrieving data is a good one, because the need to do this
occurs so frequently when running a program. The stack does
not always reside at any particular area of memory. Where it
is located is determined by the programmer, through the use of
one of the load stack pointer instructions.

    The stack is organized as a "last in - first out" or LIFO
system. When new values are "pushed" onto the stack, they are
saved "backwards" in memory, and the stack pointer is
decremented by 2. When values are "popped" out of the stack,
the SP is incremented by 2. This is why the stack pointer
usually points below its original value.   Figure   4-1
illustrates the way the stack works.

Location	Contents	Comments
7000	F3	Registers saved here if PUSH
7001	0E	operation executed.
7002	14	Current top of stack. Contents
7003	26	moved to registers if POP executed.
7004	39	Next level of stack after next POP
7005	8A	executed.
SP = 7002		Contents of stack pointer register.

Figure 4-1: Registers are saved in the stack in a "backwards"
order.   In this example, the stack pointer SP contains 7002.
If a PUSH or CALL operation is executed, register contents are
saved at 7001 and 7000, and the SP is decremented by 2.   If a
POP or RET is executed, the contents of 7002 and 7003 are
moved to registers, and the SP incremented by 2.

4.2 PUSH and POP Instructions

All uses of the stack are for double registers only. One of
the primary uses of the stack is through the PUSH and POP
instructions. PUSH saves the contents of a double register in
the stack, and POP retrieves them. You can PUSH or POP AF,
BC, DE, HL, IX, and IY. PUSH and POP instructions for the
general registers require only one byte of memory (those for
the index registers require two), and the execution of a PUSH
or POP is always faster than a load referring to a memory
location.   When the values in a register pair are pushed onto
the stack, the registers themselves are unchanged.

    Let us suppose, for example, that the SP contains 4288H.
(The "H" appended to a number means that it is hexadecimal.)
Upon executing a PUSH HL instruction, the computer saves
register H in location 4287H, L in 4286H, and leaves the SP
containing 4286H.   As with all double register saves, the
least-significant byte is followed in memory by the most-
significant byte. If this instruction were to be followed by
a POP DE, E would be loaded from 4286H and D from 4287H, and
the SP left pointing to 4288H.   Thus, the stack pointer always
contains the address from which data will be popped.

4.3 Call and Return Instructions

Another primary use of the stack pointer is with the CALL and
RETURN instructions.   (RETURN is abbreviated RET.)   You are
probably familiar with the concept behind CALLs and RETURNs
from the GOSUB and RETURN statements in Basic.   A SUBROUTINE
is a portion of a program that can be entered from different
locations,   with the ability to return to the location
immediately following the CALL when it is over.   Whenever any

Z-80 instruction is being executed, the program counter (PC) points to the NEXT instruction in memory. Thus, when the computer encounters a CALL instruction, the PC contains the return address. What happens during a CALL is that the contents of the PC are pushed onto the stack, the SP is decremented by 2, and the computer branches to the location specified. When a RETURN is executed, the address is popped off the stack, the SP is incremented by 2, and the computer branches to the address. Naturally, if the stack area is used by the subroutine, the SP must be returned to its original value before the RETURN is executed. This is one way in which inexperienced programmers frequently make errors.

Both the CALL and RET instructions of the Z-80 can be executed, unconditionally or conditionally, depending on the conditions NZ, Z, NC, C, PO, PE, P, and M. For example, CALL NZ,ADR would call the location named ADR only if the condition NZ were true, and RET NZ would return only on the same condition. These features greatly enhance the flexibility of subroutine usage with the Z-80.

4.4 Restart Instructions

The RST (restart) instructions are very similar to the CALL instructions. These one-byte instructions are, in effect, calls to locations 0 through 56 (38H) in multiples of 8. The reason for this limitation is that only 3 BITS of the address are included in the instruction itself. (A regular CALL requires 3 bytes, 2 of which contain the address called.) Unfortunately, these instructions are not as useful on the TRS-80 as they are on the Z-80 in general, because locations 0 through 56 are in ROM (although calls to them are "vectored" out of ROM as explained in chapter 5). These locations are already used extensively by the Level I and Level II Basic interpreters. What you cannot do is write a new subroutine to be loaded into these memory locations.

4.5 Miscellaneous Stack Instructions

There are several miscellaneous instructions that use the stack pointer register or the value at the top of the stack. Three instructions, "LD SP,HL", "LD SP,IX", and "LD SP,IY", set the SP to some specific value taken from one of the other 16-bit registers (HL, IX, or IY). "LD SP,nn" takes it from immediate data, and "LD SP,(nn)" takes it from a memory location. "LD (nn),SP" saves the value of the SP in a memory location. The operand SP refers to the ADDRESS of the stack area, whereas (SP) refers to the CONTENTS of the two locations at the top of the stack. "EX (SP),HL", "EX (SP),IX", and "EX

(SP),IY" swap the values at the top of the stack with the specified 16-bit registers. The SP itself is unchanged by these operations. "INC SP" increments the stack pointer, and "DEC SP" decrements it. The stack area is also used to save registers during interrupt processing, but we will not discuss that here.

4.6 Subroutines

The stack has numerous applications in practically every Z-80 program. The most important of these is undoubtedly the establshment and use of subroutines. Subroutines should ALWAYS be used when a particular sequence of operations is to be repeated from more than one location within a program. The CALL to the subroutine and its associated RET require only four bytes and 27 machine cycles to execute. The only conditions that warrant not using a subroutine are that the operations require four bytes or less, or that the execution timing is so critical that you cannot spare the 27 machine cycles (about 15 microseconds).

If you need to use a register in which to carry out some operation, but you also need to retain its present contents, you can PUSH it onto the stack and POP it off afterwards. For example, suppose that a subroutine needs to use HL as a scratch register, but needs to return with the present contents of HL unchanged. There are two general solutions to this problem:

```
            CALL  SUB
            ...
      SUB   PUSH  HL
            ...
            POP   HL
            RET
```

or:

```
            PUSH  HL
            CALL  SUB
            POP   HL
```

In other words, the PUSH and POP can occur either in the subroutine (usually preferable, since the registers will be saved for any call) or in the calling program, but they must occur at the same program level. What you must NOT do is the following:

```
              PUSH   HL
              CALL   SUB
              ...
       SUB    POP    HL
```

or:

```
              CALL   SUB
              POP    HL
              ...
       SUB    PUSH   HL
```

In these examples, the SP gets confused because the PUSH and POP do not occur at the same level. The first example POPs the return address off the stack rather than the previous contents of HL, and the second pushes HL onto the stack, so that the program will "return" to the address specified by HL rather than the calling location. Of course, these programming techniques can be used if the programmer understands what is happening and takes that into account when writing the program, so that something he intends to happen occurs. The point is that these are not proper procedures for storing and retrieving registers.

Another use of PUSH and POP is simply to transfer data from one register pair to another. The following two sequences of instructions produce the same result:

```
              PUSH   DE
              POP    HL
```

and:

```
              LD     H,D
              LD     L,E
```

Both require two bytes, and, although the latter method requires only 8 T cycles and the former 22, programmers are as likely to use one method as the other. Using PUSH and POP also allows data to be transferred to and from the index registers, and it allows access to the flags for such purposes as printing them.

If several registers are PUSHed at the beginning of a subroutine, they must be POPped at the end in REVERSE order; otherwise the data will not go back into the same registers. The following sequence shows the correct procedure:

```
SUB     PUSH    AF
        PUSH    BC
        PUSH    DE
        PUSH    HL
        ...
        POP     HL
        POP     DE
        POP     BC
        POP     AF
        RET
```

None of the stack operations affects the condition codes
except for POP AF, which loads the flag register with an
entirely different set of conditions. Therefore, the values
of registers can be restored before a conditional operation,
as in the following sequence:

```
PUSH    DE          ;save D (and E)
LD      D,(TST)     ;load D from TST
CP      D           ;compare A to D
POP     DE          ;restore DE to previous values
CALL    Z,SUB       ;call if compare equal
```

(In assembly code, anything following a semi-colon is taken to
be a comment.) This small portion of a program saves D and E
in the stack and then loads D from a location called TST.
This is compared to the accumulator, and then registers D and
E are popped back off the stack. The CALL is executed only if
the compare was equal, but by the time the CALL occurs, D and
E have been restored to their previous values.

     Since all subroutines use the same stack area, any time a
RET is executed it will branch to the address at the top of
the stack, regardless of which program executed the last CALL.
Assuming that SUB2 is a subroutine that ends in a RET (as all
subroutines do), the following program sequences are
identical:

```
SUB1    ...
        CALL    SUB2
        RET
```

and:

```
SUB1    ...
        JP      SUB2
```

The first SUB1 sequence CALLs SUB2; SUB2 does its thing and
returns to SUB1; and SUB1 returns to the calling program.
The second SUB1 sequence ends by jumping to SUB2; when SUB2
returns, it goes back to the program that called SUB1.

What happens if a program tries to call itself?   Imagine this:

                5000   CALL   5000

Location 5000 contains the first byte of an instruction that calls location 5000! When executed, 5003 (the return address) is pushed onto the stack, the SP is decremented, and the computer branches to 5000. Then 5003 is again pushed onto the stack, and the process continues. This program will have the effect of repeatedly pushing 5003 onto the stack, thus destroying all of memory and causing the computer to hang indefinitely. Actually, the process will continue until location 5000 is bombed, and then the computer will repeatedly execute the instructions represented by 50 (LD D,B) and 03 (INC BC).

Because the use of the stack is so flexible, you never need to worry about where to store data temporarily. Just push it onto the stack. Always make sure that you know where the stack is located so that you don't use it for other data. The best way to accomplish this is always to put a load stack pointer instruction at the beginning of any program you write. And don't forget that the computer also uses the stack during subroutine calls and interrupts, so that you have to keep PUSHes and POPs on the same levels.

5

MEMORY MAP

Before you can write an assembly-language program for the TRS-80, you must know the organization of the TRS-80's memory and how to use the various parts of it. Most TRS-80 owners are familiar with the division of the memory into ROM (read-only memory), dedicated input/output addresses, and RAM (random access memory), as shown in the diagram on the following page. In this chapter, we will examine each of these three memory areas in detail.

The ROM contains the Level II Basic interpreter, as well as the software for accessing the principal input/output devices -- the keyboard, video display, and cassette recorder. The main reason for placing software in ROM is so that you cannot accidentally erase it.

The dedicated input/output addresses contain locations where certain devices are interfaced to the TRS-80 through MEMORY MAPPING. Only the keyboard, video display, line printer, disk controller, and cassette recorder are connected in this way. (The cassette recorder also uses port 255.) Additional devices can be interfaced through I/O ports.

The RAM is where your programs and data must be located, but many addresses at the bottom of RAM are reserved for special purposes. In a non-disk Level II Basic system, 744

DECIMAL ADDRESS	HEXADECIMAL ADDRESS	
Ø	ØH	LEVEL II BASIC ROM (LEVEL I ENDS AT 4095 = ØFFFH)
12287	2FFFH	
12288	3ØØØH	DEDICATED I/O ADDRESSES
16383	3FFFH	
16384	4ØØØH	RAM
20479	4FFFH	END OF 4 K RAM
20480	5ØØØH	
32767	7FFFH	END OF 16K RAM
32768	8ØØØH	
49151	BFFFH	END OF 32K RAM
49152	CØØØH	
05535	FFFFH	END OF 48K RAM

Figure 2: Memory map

locations are reserved. When you connect a disk drive to the TRS-8Ø, the software needed to operate the disk must be loaded off the system drive into low RAM. This area of RAM then functions as an extension of the ROM, and if you accidentally destroy it, you must reboot the system. The TRSDOS disk operating system reserves over 5K, and Disk Basic requires an additional 5K.

5.1   The Level II Basic ROM

The TRS-8Ø has an unusually large ROM for a microcomputer. Most micros have just some kind of monitor or operating system in ROM, containing only the software for accessing the primary input/output devices. The TRS-8Ø has all that, but it also has the Level II Basic interpreter, which is huge by comparison. Level II Basic is an extremely complicated assembly-language program, written by Microsoft. Understanding how it works is beyond the scope of this book and unnecessary. Most of the Level II interpreter is unusable to assembly-language programs, although in chapter 15 we discuss assembly-language subroutines for Basic programs.

The primary information we need to know about the ROM concerns the input/output software. We may also be interested in knowing the general organization of Level II Basic, and how to find out more about it. The general organization of the Level II ROM is as follows (all addresses are in hexa-decimal):

```
0000 - 01D8      System initialization and I/O subroutines
01D9 - 03E2      Cassette subroutines
03E3 - 0457      Keyboard driver
0458 - 058C      Video display driver
058D - 0673      Line-printer driver
0674 - 070A      Initialization code
070B - 1607      Floating-point math
1608 - 164F      Table of entry points for functions
1650 - 1820      Level II Basic reserved words
1821 - 1899      Table of entry points for Level II commands
189A - 18C8      Unknown
18C9 - 18F6      Non-DOS error messages
18F7 - 191C      Non-DOS initialization
191D - 1953      Messages
1936 - 2FFF      Remaining Level II interpreter
```

The ROM contains an enormous number of subroutines, but few of them are useful for assembly-language programs. Those that are useful are summarized below. This list shows the entry point (in hexadecimal), the registers containing parameters for the subroutine, the registers used (destroyed), and the operation of the subroutine. (Subroutines are always entered by a CALL instruction.)

5.2 Keyboard Subroutines

002BH   INKEY subroutine: scans the keyboard and returns
         zero in A if no key is depressed, else returns a
         character. Uses AF, DE.

0049H   INPUT subroutine: scans the keyboard and waits for a
         key to be depressed. Returns character in A.
         Uses AF, DE.

0040H   LINE INPUT subroutine: accepts an entire line of
         input terminated by ENTER or BREAK. Displays
         characters typed, recognizing control functions
         (backspace, etc.). When called, HL => address of
         buffer where text is to be put, B = maximum number
         of characters in line. On exit, B = number of
         characters typed, including terminator. C set if
         line ends with BREAK. Uses AF, DE.

5.3 Video Display Subroutines

0033H   DISPLAY subroutine: prints ASCII character in A
         at current cursor position on video display. Cursor
         located at 4020H. Uses AF, DE, IY.

Ø1C9H   CLEAR SCREEN subroutine: Clears screen and homes
         cursor. Uses AF.

28A7H   TEXT PRINT subroutine: prints all text pointed to
         by HL up to a carriage return (ENTER key = ØDH) or
         NULL (ØØ) at current cursor position. Uses HL, AF.

                    5.4 Cassette Subroutines

Ø212H   DEFINE DRIVE: selects cassette and turns motor on.
         A=Ø for cassette #1, or 1 for cassette #2. Uses AF.

Ø1F8H   CASSETTE OFF subroutine. Uses no parameters.

Ø287H   Write leader and sync byte. Uses AF, C.

Ø264H   Write byte in A to cassette.

Ø296H   Read leader and sync byte: locates beginning of
         program and positions for reading next bytes. Motor
         keeps running. Uses AF.

Ø235H   Read byte: next byte on cassette returned in A.
         User must keep up with cassette speed of 5ØØ baud.

    Since   all   the   standard   TRS-8Ø tapes,   such   as   Basic
programs, machine-language object programs, and Basic data
tapes, are written in special formats, you need additional
information to use the cassette. This subject is covered in
detail in chapter 14.

              5.5 Miscellaneous I/O Subroutines

ØØ3BH   LINE PRINT subroutine: prints byte in A on line
         printer. On exit, Z is set if printer is ready.
         Uses AF, DE.

ØØ13H   Inputs a byte from an input device. On entry, DE =>
         DCB of device. On exit, Z is set if ready. Uses AF.

ØØ1BH   Output a byte to a device. On entry, A=output byte,
         DE => DCB of device. On exit, Z is set if device is
         ready. Uses AF.

ØØ23H   Output a control byte to an I/O device. On entry,
         A = control byte, DE => DCB of device. On exit, Z is
         set if device is ready, A = status. Uses AF.

0060H   Delay loop in 14.66-microsecond increments.
         BC = number of delay pulses. Uses AF, BC.

0066H   NMI reset location: jumps here on non-maskable
         interrupt. In effect, halt or reset.

5.6 RST vectors

You may recall from our discussion of the Z-80 instruction set
above that the RST instructions have the same effect as a CALL
to locations 0 to 56 in multiples of 8. It may appear that
you cannot use these instructions, because the area that they
call is in ROM. Actually, you can use most of them, because
calls to these locations are vectored out into low RAM
addresses.   These addresses contain jumps to yet another
series of addresses that are automatically inserted there by
power on or reset. (A "vector" is simply a jump instruction.)
Nevertheless, all of the restart instructions are   used
extensively by Level II Basic, so you must take this into
account when setting up your own routines. RST 0-32 are used
by Level II, and RST 40-56 by Disk Basic and DOS only. The
operation of RST 48 and RST 56 is too complicated to describe
in the summary here.   The following table shows the vector
addresses and gives a brief description of the   Basic
function:

RST decimal	RST hex	Jumps to	Vector	Function
0	0H	(none)	(none)	Reboot system: power on or reset.
8	8H	4000H	1C96H	Byte at HL compared with byte at top of stack. If non-zero, SN error.
16	10H	4003H	1D78H	Increment HL and pass through string, ignoring spaces or carriage return. C is set if next character numeric, else C is reset.
24	18H	4006H	1C90H	HL compared to DE. Z is set if equal, C set if DE>HL.
32	20H	4009H	25D9H	If double-precision number C is reset, else C is set.
40	28H	400CH	4BA2H	BREAK key vector: jumps here if BREAK key is typed.
48	30H	400FH	44B4H	
56	38H	4012H	4518H	

5/7 Level II Basic Commands

The Level II ROM map shown above does not go into the decoding of Basic statements. If you are interested in this subject, the following information will explain how to find out more about it.

Each of the Level II Basic reserved words is represented internally by a unique byte, called a "token", with a value from 80H to FBH. When you type in a Basic program, only the tokens are stored -- not the complete words you type. Starting at location 1650H and extending to 1820H is a list of all the reserved words, in numerical order of the tokens. The first byte of each word is indicated by having bit 7 set, which is not used in ASCII code. There are two tables of jump addresses, located at 1608H - 164FH and 1822H - 1899H, plus a third area starting around 24B0H, that give the addresses where each command is executed. If you figure all this out, you will construct the following table, which is shown by tokens, in alphabetical order rather than numerical:

Word	Token	Addr	Word	Token	Addr	Word	Token	Addr
ABS	D9	0977	GOSUB	91	1EB1	READ	8B	21EF
AND	D2	25FD	GOTO	8D	1EC2	REM	93	1F07
ASC	F6	2A0F	IF	8F	2039	RESET	82	0138
ATN	E4	15BD	INKEY$	C9	019D	RESTORE	90	1D91
AUTO	B7	2008	INP	DB	2AEF	RESUME	9F	1FAF
CDBL	F1	0ADB	INPUT	89	219A	RETURN	92	1EDE
CHR$	F7	2A1F	INSTR	C5	419D	RIGHT$	F9	2A91
CINT	EF	0A7F	INT	D8	0B37	RND	DE	14C9
CLEAR	B8	1E7A	KILL	AA	4191	RSET	AC	419A
CLOAD	B9	2C1F	LEFT$	F8	2A61	RUN	8E	1EA3
CLOSE	A6	4185	LEN	F3	2A03	SAVE	AD	41A0
CLS	84	01C9	LET	8C	1F21	SET	83	0135
CMD	85	4173	LINE	9C	41A3	SGN	D7	098A
CONT	B3	1DE4	LIST	B4	2B2E	SIN	E2	1547
COS	E1	1541	LLIST	B5	2B29	SQR	DD	13E7
CSAVE	BA	2BF5	LOAD	A7	4188	STEP	CC	2B01
CSNG	F0	0AB1	LOC	EA	4164	STOP	94	1DA9
CVD	E8	415E	LOF	EB	4167	STR$	F4	2836
CVI	E6	4152	LOG	DF	0809	STRING$	C4	2A2F
CVS	E7	4158	LPRINT	AF	2067	SYSTEM	AE	02B2
DATA	88	1F05	LSET	AB	4197	TAB(	BC	2137
DEF	B0	415B	MEM	C8	27C9	TAN	E3	15A8
DEFDBL	9B	1E09	MERGE	A8	418B	THEN	CA	----
DEFINT	99	1E03	MID$	FA	2A9A	TIME$	C7	4176
DEFSNG	9A	1E06	MKD$	EE	4170	TO	BD	----
DEFSTR	98	1E00	MKI$	EC	416A	TROFF	97	1DF8
DELETE	B6	2BC6	MKS$	ED	416D	TRON	96	1DF7
DIM	8A	2608	NAME	A9	418E	USING	BF	2CBD
EDIT	9D	2E60	NEW	BB	1B49	USR	C1	27FE
ELSE	95	1F07	NEXT	87	22B6	VAL	F5	2AC5

END	80	1DAE	NOT	CB	25C4	VARPTR	C0	24EB
EOF	E9	4161	ON	A1	1F6C	+	CD	249F
ERL	C2	24DD	OPEN	A2	4179	−	CE	2532
ERR	C3	24CF	OR	D3	25F7	*	CF	----
ERROR	9E	1FF4	OUT	A0	2AFB	/	D0	----
EXP	E0	1439	PEEK	E5	2CAA	**	D1	----
FIELD	A3	417C	POINT	C6	0132	>	D4	----
FIX	F2	0B26	POKE	B1	2CB1	=	D5	----
FN	BE	4155	POS	DC	27F5	<	D6	----
FOR	81	1CA1	PRINT	B2	206F	'	FB	----
FRE	DA	27D4	PUT	A5	4182	"	22	2866
GET	A4	417F	RANDOM	86	01D3	&	26	4194
						.	2E	0E6C

** Indicates the up arrow key.

     If you want to know more about the ROM, the best thing to
do is to get a disassembler program and look at a disassembled
listing of the ROM. A disassembler is the reverse of an
assembler, showing the machine instructions corresponding to
the program stored in memory.

     One final word of caution about the ROM is in order: there
are different versions of the ROM that are and have been sold
by Radio Shack. All of the ROMs are functionally identical,
but exactly what the differences are and why different ROMs
are being sold are not known at the time of this writing.

                  5.8   Dedicated I/O Addresses

The area from 3000H to 3FFFH is used for direct-memory-access
(DMA) input/output devices. It is organized as follows:

3000 - 37DD	Unused at present
37E0	Disk drive select latch
	(37DE, 37DF, 37E1-37E7 also used for disk)
37E4	Cassette drive select latch
	(cassette also uses port FF)
37E8	Line printer
37EC - 37EF	Disk controller
3800 - 3880	Keyboard addressing
3C00 - 3FFF	Video display memory

     Since the keyboard and video display are so important for
the functioning of the TRS-80, their operation will be
explained in more detail.

5.9 Keyboard Addressing

Locations 3800H - 3BFFH do not exist in the TRS-80's memory. When a location there is addressed, the computer actually reads the keys of the keyboard. Each key depressed causes a certain bit in a specific location to read "1" rather than "0". The correspondence between the keys and the memory locations is as follows:

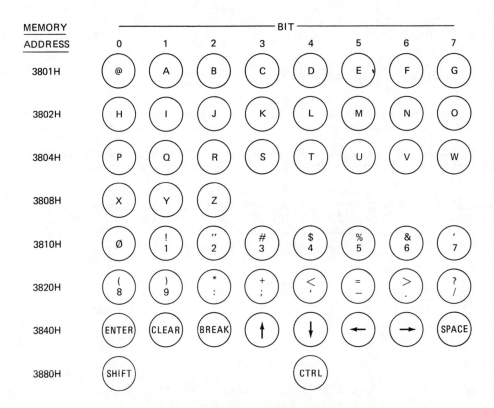

Figure 3: Keyboard addressing

For example, if you type the "F" key, bit 6 in location 3801 will be set, causing the value at 3801 to read 40H. A keyboard-reading subroutine must simply check locations 3801 to 3840 to see if there is any non-zero value, and then decode the bits into the proper letter, checking location 3880H to see if the shift or control keys are pressed. This may seem like much work, but it actually happens so fast that a keyboard-debounce routine has become necessary to prevent

accidental double reading of typed letters.   The keyboard
debounce   does   nothing   except   insert   a   delay   into   the
key-reading process.

                5.10   Video Display Memory

The video display memory occupies   locations   3C00H - 3FFFH.
This is a 1K buffer that is mapped directly to the 1024
positions of the video display,   starting   in   the   upper-left
corner and extending 64 characters across each line for 16
lines.   If you store a number in one of these   locations,   its
ASCII   equivalent   is   displayed on the screen.   (ASCII tables
are in the LEVEL II BASIC REFERENCE MANUAL, the   EDITOR/ASSEM-
BLER REFERENCE MANUAL, and the TRSDOS & DISK BASIC REFERENCE
MANUAL.) Unless your TRS-80 has   been   modified   to   display
lower-case letters, bit 6 of the video display memory does not
exist.

    If you store a value in video memory that has bit 7 set, it
indicates a graphics character.   Graphics divide   each   cursor
position   into   six   PIXELS.   Bits 0-5 of the value stored
determine which pixels are set.   These bits   are   mapped   into
the graphics as follows:

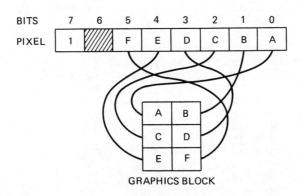

BITS   7   6   5   4   3   2   1   0
PIXEL | 1 |///| F | E | D | C | B | A |

                    | A | B |
                    | C | D |
                    | E | F |

                GRAPHICS BLOCK

                4: Graphics

                5.11   The RAM

As   we   mentioned above, a minimum of 744 bytes of low RAM are
reserved for Level II Basic, and approximately 10K is used   in
Disk Basic. All of your programs and data must go elsewhere.
It is important to have an understanding of what is located in
these   reserved   addresses.   Some   of them are used by every
TRS-80 program, whereas others are used only by obscure Basic

commands. Even adding Disk Basic to the system does not complicate matters that much, for the DOS is loaded from 4400H, and all you need to know is that it functions as an extension of the ROM, so you shouldn't destroy it. Different disk operating systems use the memory immediately below this area in different ways, some of which are incompatible with other DOSs.

The data control blocks (DCBs) for the three primary I/O devices of the TRS-80 are located immediately following the jump vectors. These blocks are the keyboard, video display, and line printer. The concept behind a DCB is very intelligent, and the fact that it is in RAM is also important, because it enables you to use different software from that in the ROM. The organization of all DCBs is very similar:

Byte 1:	DCB type
Bytes 2-3:	driver address
Bytes 4-6:	parameters used by the device
Bytes 7-8:	identifying letters

The "driver" for each device is the software that actually stores or fetches data from it. By patching a different address pointing to a different driver into these bytes, you can use non-standard software, such as the keyboard-debounce routine. When additional devices are added to the TRS-80, they are often also interfaced through DCBs.

The following table shows the complete organization of low RAM. All addresses are in hexadecimal. The functions of addresses which are not indicated are unknown.

```
4000              RST 8    Jump vectors for RST instructions
4003              RST 16
4006              RST 24
4009              RST 32
400C              RST 40
400F              RST 48
4012              RST 56
4015 - 401C       Keyboard DCB
4016              ROM driver address: 03E3H
401B              Device name KI ("keyboard input")
401D - 4024       Video display DCB
401E              ROM driver address: 0458H
4020              Cursor location
4022              Cursor character
4023              Device name DO ("display output")
4025 - 402C       Line printer DCB
4026              ROM driver address 058DH
4028              Lines/page
4029              Line counter
```

```
402B                    Device name PR ("printer")
402D                    Normal return to DOS
4030                    Error return to DOS
4036 - 403C             Keyboard work area
403D                    Print-size flag (0=64 char, 8=32 char mode)
4040                    25-msec heartbeat interrupt
4041 - 4046             TIME$ storage area
4041                    Time: seconds, minutes, hours
4044                    Date: year, day, month
4047                    Lowest location of usable memory
4049                    Highest location of usable memory
4050                    FDC interrupt vector
4052                    Communications interrupt vector
4054 - 405C             Reserved
408E                    Entry point to USR routines
4093                    INP (input port) routine
4096                    OUT (output port) routine
4099                    INKEY$ storage
409A                    Error code storage for RESUME
409B                    Printer-carriage position
409C                    Device-type flag: -1=tape, 0=video, 1=printer
409D                    PRINT# use
40A0                    Start-of-string space pointer
40A4                    Start-of-Basic program pointer
40A6                    Line-cursor position, used for TAB
40A7                    Input-buffer pointer
40AA - 40AC             Seed for RND
40AF                    Number type flag (NTR):  2=integer,
                        3=string, 4=single, 8=double
40B1                    Top of Basic memory pointer
40B3                    String work-area pointer
40B5 - 40D5             String work area
40D6                    Memory size pointer
40DC                    Used by DIM
40DE                    Used by PRINT USING
40DF                    System tape entry-point storage
40E1                    Auto flag:  0=not auto, else auto
40E2                    Line number
40E4                    Auto increment
40E6                    Encoded-statement pointer
40E8                    Pointer-to-stack pointer
40EA                    Used by RESUME
40EC                    Edit line number
40EE                    Used by RESUME
40F5                    Last line number executed
40F7                    Used by CONT
40F9                    Pointer to end of Basic program
                        Also simple-variables pointer
40FB                    Arrays pointer
40FD - 4100             Free space
```

```
4101 - 411A        Variable type declaration table (A-Z)
                   2=integer, 3=string, 4=single, 8=double
411B               TRON flag: 0=TROFF
411D - 4124        Arith table
4127 - 412E        Arithex table
4130               Line-number work area pointer
4152 - 41A5        DOS entry points
4152               CVI
4155               FN
4158               CVS
415B               DEF
415E               CVD
4161               EOF
4164               LOC
4167               LOF
416A               MKI$
416D               MKS$
4170               MKD$
4173               CMD
4176               TIME$
4179               OPEN
417C               FIELD
417F               GET
4182               PUT
4185               CLOSE
4188               LOAD
418B               MERGE
418E               NAME
4191               KILL
4194               &
4197               LSET
419A               RSET
419D               INSTR
41A0               SAVE
41A3               LINE
41E8 - 42E7        Input-buffer area
4288               System stack pointer
42E8               Always zero
42E9               Start of Basic program
                   (Disk Basic programs start at 68BA)
```

While Basic programs start at location 42E9H, pressing the
reset button causes material to be written into locations
4330H through 4348H, thus making 4349H the first free location
for assembly language programs. When running a Disk system,
7000H is the first free location used neither by Disk Basic
nor by the TRSDOS utilities.

6

USING THE
EDITOR/ASSEMBLER
PROGRAM

When you think you are finally beginning to understand the machine instructions for the TRS-80 and are ready to try writing a program to do something, then you have to consider the problem of getting the instructions into the computer. This is where the Editor/Assembler program comes into play.

The Editor/Assembler program was one of the first software packages sold by Radio Shack. Developed by Microsoft, the company that wrote Level II Basic, the original program came with a very helpful book called the TRS-80 EDITOR/ASSEMBLER USER INSTRUCTION MANUAL (catalog number 26-2002). This book is perhaps the most important book anyone planning to write assembly-language programs for the TRS-80 should read. It is not easy reading, however, and most beginners will get confused by its rather clumsy organization and lack of sufficient introductory explanatory material.

One drawback of the original Editor/Assembler program, which we will henceforth refer to by its shorthand name EDTASM, was that it allowed programs to be saved only on the cassette-tape recorder. This worked fine, but it took a long time to read tapes into the computer. A revised version of EDTASM has been available with Apparat's NEWDOS PLUS which extends the input-output routines so that they work with either cassette or disk. This program has a number of other improvements over the original. Microsoft has also introduced a similar revision called Editor/Assembler plus, and many other assemblers are now available. Whether you have the tape or disk version, however, the EDTASM program is identical in all other respects.

When you write an assembly-language program, you have in mind a specific series of machine instructions that you want to have loaded into the computer at some particular memory address, and then executed. There are actually several steps involved in this process. Let us try to clarify these steps and introduce some terminology.

The machine instructions to be executed must be written down in some kind of notation. They are indicated individually by names called "mnemonics" (pronounced "nem-on-iks"). The mnemonics used by the EDTASM program are the Zilog names introduced above in chapter 3. There are other sets of mnemonics that have been designed for the Z-80 (mostly as extensions of 8080 mnemonics) that are rather different from the Zilog notation, but we will not mention them because we won't be using them.

The starting location in memory at which we want to have the program assembled is called the "origin" of the program. This is indicated to the assembler by the ORG pseudo-operation. ORG is called a "pseudo-operation" because it is not a machine instruction. There are several other pseudo-operations, such as the END statement, which indicates the end of the program. The function of a pseudo-op is to indicate something to the assembler other than a machine instruction.

The function of the assembler is to translate the mnemonics that indicate your program into the numerical values that represent the operations you have specified. Each instruction is denoted by a unique value for a byte or series of bytes. Z-80 instructions may be 1 to 4 bytes long. For example, 04 indicates "INC B" (increment the B register), and 3E, the first byte of a 2-byte instruction, indicates "LD A,N" (load A with the value specified in the next byte). These values are referred to as "machine code", and a particular sequence of instructions that perform some task is a program. The important point here is that every instruction corresponds to a number, and the assembler's function is to translate your mnemonics into those numbers.

The numbers that represent instructions are only one kind of numerical value handled by the assembler. Others include data values and addresses. Numerical data values are self-defining. "3" indicates the value 3. The only possible confusion is the number system employed. EDTASM's convention is that all numbers are decimal unless followed by the letters

H or O, in which case they are either hexadecimal (base 16) or
octal (base 8).   "30" indicates the value 30, but "30H"
indicates 30 hexadecimal, which is 48 decimal. Addresses and
machine code are always printed in hexadecimal form by the
assembler.

Addresses, which are always two-byte values, indicate the
memory locations at which either the machine instructions or
data they employ are located.   When the program is being
assembled, an internal number called the "location counter" is
set equal to the value you specify as the origin of the
program.   As each instruction is assembled, the location
counter is incremented by the number of bytes in the
instruction.   You can refer to the location counter by the
symbol "$", to which you can add or subtract values.   For
example, the instruction "JP $+5" indicates a jump to the
location 5 bytes ahead of the value of the location counter at
the beginning of the JP instruction. When using the location
counter, it is necessary to count the number of bytes
corresponding to each instruction between the "$" and the
location referred to. You must always jump to the first byte
of an instruction.   Otherwise, a disastrous error could
occur.

Addresses are usually referred to by "labels", which are
symbolic names of one to six letters, written at the beginning
of a program line. When you are writing a program, you do not
normally think about such problems as how many bytes fit
between the area where you are currently writing down your
instructions and something you are referring to. When you use
a label, the assembler computes the appropriate value
corresponding to the label and substitutes it for every
reference to it within the program.

When your program is written out in mnemonic form, it is
called a "source program". Once it has been assembled into
machine code, it is called an "object program".   The
assembler's function is to translate your source program into
an object program, and then to store the results either on
cassette or disk, from which it can be read into memory. The
assembler can also store your source program in symbolic form
on cassette or disk, and read it back in later. What we need
to understand here is that reading the program into memory is
another step, called "loading", which must be done after the
assembly is finished. This will be done either with the
SYSTEM command in Basic if the program is stored on cassette,
or with the LOAD or RUN commands in TRSDOS if stored on disk.

6.1   Editor/Assembler Commands

Assembling the program is only half the job of the EDTASM program.   The other half of its name is "Editor".   This means that EDTASM also contains a text editor, which you use when typing your program into the computer.   The Editor is simple and easy to use.   All commands are single letters.   To type in your program, you use the I (Insert) command, unless you are replacing an existing line, in which case you use R (Replace). I works very much like the AUTO command in Basic.   Every line in the program has a line number, but you don't have to type the number.   It is printed automatically.   The default first line number is 100, and 10 is the default increment between each line, enabling you to insert up to 9 lines between each existing line.   If you need to insert more, you must first renumber the lines with the N (Number) command, which takes no more than about a second.   While typing the program, the right arrow can be used as a Tab key, which jumps in groups of eight spaces.

A group of several successive lines can be indicated by separating the first and last numbers by a colon.   This is necessary with several commands, such as D (Delete), P (Print), or H (Hardcopy).   ("Hardcopy" means "line print", while "print" goes to the video display.)   The symbols "#" and "*" can be used in place of the first and last lines, and "." in place of the current line.   For example, D100:120 deletes lines 100 through 120.   P#:* prints the entire program on the video display.

Once a line has been typed in, you can modify it with the E (Edit) command.   Edit works exactly the same way as the EDIT command in Level II Basic.   In addition to Edit, there is an F (Find) command that searches through the entire program for a particular string.   If you want to change each occurrence of it, however, you must do so one-at-a-time.

An entire source program can be saved on tape, or in the revised EDTASM, on disk.   This is done by the W (Write) command, while reading in a previously-stored program is done by L (Load).

Finally, there is the most important command, A (Assemble). A has several options, which can be specified in any combination, separated by slashes.   The first string following A (and a space) is the name of the object program (this is used only if the program is written to cassette).   Other options are NO (no object tape or file written), NS (no symbol table printed), LP (line print: assembly printed on line printer rather than video display), NL (no listing: assembles without printing), and WE (wait on error: pauses whenever an error occurs). For example, to assemble your program you might specify: "A PROG/WE/NS" meaning "assemble the program now typed into memory, wait if any error occurs, and don't print a symbol table at the end."

There is one other command: B (Basic), which returns you to Level II Basic, or to TRSDOS if you have a disk.

During the assembly process, your source program is stored in memory, and the symbol table, which consists of all the labels you have used and the addresses where they occur, is stored backwards starting at the top end of memory. The most discouraging error you can get is "SYMBOL TABLE OVERFLOW", which means that you don't have enough memory to contain the program and assemble it. Before giving up, however, you can eliminate your comments and try again.

When you are typing in a program, each line has four different fields, three of which are optional. The format is as follows:

    (LABEL)   OPCODE   (OPERAND(S))   (;COMMENTS)

Optional fields are indicated as being enclosed in parentheses. Each field is separated by either a space, or preferably by the right-arrow key, which aligns the fields vertically. The comments must be preceded by a semi-colon, and an entire line may be comments if it begins with a semi-colon. The LABEL is a symbol whose value is set equal to the location counter when the line is assembled. The OPCODE is the mnemonic for the instruction. The OPERAND(S) indicate the registers or values used by the opcode, but not all opcodes have operands. COMMENTS are for your own benefit, so that you can remember what you are doing.

6.2 Writing a Program

Now that we have described the Editor, let us try to go over the process of writing a program. In the EDTASM manual there is an example program that consists of just three steps: first, it fills the entire video screen with a graphics block. Second, it waits a few seconds to leave the screen "whited out". Finally, it returns to Basic or TRSDOS. We will go over this program step-by-step, and explain what it does and how it does it. The program is as follows:

```
00100                 ORG      7000H
00110      VIDEO      EQU      3C00H
00120      START      LD       HL,VIDEO          ;SOURCE ADDRESS
00130                 LD       DE,VIDEO+1        ;DEST. ADDRESS
```

```
00140              LD      BC,400H        ;BYTE COUNT
00150              LD      (HL),0BFH      ;GRAPHICS BYTE
00160              LDIR                   ;WRITE OUT SCREEN
00170      ;DELAY LOOP TO KEEP WHITED-OUT SCREEN ON
00180              LD      B,5
00190     LP1      LD      HL,0FFFFH      ;VALUE TO DECREMENT
00200     LP2      DEC     HL
00210              LD      A,H
00220              OR      L              ;HL=0?
00230              JP      NZ,LP2         ;IF NO DEC AGAIN
00240              DJNZ    LP1            ;DEC.B--B=0?
00250              JP      0H             ;RETURN TO BASIC
00260              END     START
00270     <BREAK>
```

This listing is taken directly from the EDTASM User's Manual. The only changes we have made are to name the first location in the program "START", to include this name on the END statement, and to change the origin of the program to 7000H so that it will work with both cassette and disk systems. (The reason for this is explained below.) The comments are those that are in the manual.

The video display is a memory-mapped output device that automatically displays whatever characters are placed in locations 3C00 to 3FFF hexadecimal (15360 to 16383). The character whose value is 0BF hexadecimal (191) is a totally white graphics symbol. If you place this character in each of the locations 3C00 to 3FFF, you will "white-out" the screen. This could be done by the following Basic program:

```
10 FOR I=15360 TO 16383
20 POKE I,191
30 NEXT I
```

One way of performing these operations in machine language would be as follows:

```
00100              LD      HL,15360       ;first loc. of screen
00110              LD      BC,1024        ;chars. on screen
00120              LD      D,191          ;graphics byte to D
00130     LOOP     LD      (HL),D         ;store D in memory
00140              INC     HL             ;point to next loc.
00150              DEC     BC             ;decrement count
00160              LD      A,B            ;BC=0?
00170              OR      C
00180              JR      NZ,LOOP        ;if non-zero, continue
```

The first three instructions load various registers with initial values, but each of the values means something quite different.   HL is 15360, the first location of the video

memory. BC is 1024, a count of the number of bytes on the
screen. D is 191, the graphics byte that we want to display.
LD (HL),D means that the value in register D is stored in the
location whose address is in the HL register pair. (We used
register D rather than A for this purpose, because A is being
used later in the program, and its value would be destroyed.)
Following this instruction, we increment HL, so that we point
to the next location in video memory, and we also decrement
BC, so that our count is decreased. Whenever a register pair
contains an address of some memory location, we say that it
"points to" that location. There are many instructions that
load or store a byte in the accumulator using a register pair
as a pointer. When this occurs, the register pair is enclosed
in parentheses.

Now comes a slightly more complicated portion of the
program. We want to know if BC is zero yet, for if it is we
are finished. However, there is no Z-80 instruction that
tests to see if a double register is zero. We must therefore
use a group of instructions. "LD A,B" loads the accumulator
with the contents of the B register. Then we perform a
logical OR operation on A with the contents of C. (Why
couldn't we use B? Because you can do arithmetic and logical
operations only in A, or HL for 2-byte operations.) OR looks
at the value of each bit in each register, and if either of
them is 1, the result is then a 1. Thus, A will be zero only
if both B and C are zero. This type of "programming quickie"
takes a long time to figure out the first time you do it, but
can be used thereafter without your having to think it through
again. The final instruction, "JR NZ,LOOP", jumps to LOOP
only if A is non-zero, repeating the process until the entire
video display is blanked out.

If you now look at the original program, you will see that
the above method was not used. Instead, the program used four
"LD" instructions and an "LDIR". The first statement, "VIDEO
EQU 3C00H", means that the value of 3C00H (15360) will be
substituted for any occurrence of the symbol VIDEO; 3C01H
(15361) is substituted for "VIDEO+1". EQU is another
pseudo-operation.

The instructions following the EQU are all in preparation
for the LDIR at the end. LDIR is one of the fanciest
instructions on any microcomputer. It is a block transfer
which uses HL as the source pointer, DE as the destination
pointer, and BC as the count. When executed, it does all of
the following: load the location pointed to by DE with the
value of the location pointed to by HL (in other words, copy
the value of (HL) to (DE)), and decrement BC. If BC is
non-zero, both HL and DE are incremented and the process is
repeated until BC is zero. LDIR is normally thought of as

moving one block of data to another block, but here the two
blocks are separated by only one byte. That is why it is
necessary to have the "LD (HL),0BFH" before LDIR. What it
does is to load 3C00 with the value 0BFH, so that when LDIR
begins (HL) contains that value. Once stored in the next
location and HL and DE are incremented, HL will continue to
point to a location containing 0BFH.

    The next portion of the example contains the delay loop. A
delay loop is usually implemented by simply loading a value
into a register and decrementing it until it is zero. If you
figure out how long it takes each instruction in the loop to
excute (a few microseconds) and multiply this by the count,
you can compute the delay time. In the actual program, there
are two delay loops, one inside the other. One of the loops
uses the HL register pair and the other the single register B.
The loops include lines 180 through 240 in the first listing
above.

    The inner loop (lines 200-230) uses the same method we
described above for testing whether the value in HL is zero:
A is loaded from H, and L is ORed to A. If the result is
non-zero, the decrementing continues. The original value in
HL is FFFF (65535), the maximum value that can be contained in
a register. It is necessary to indicate this as "0FFFFH",
because the assembler requires any hexadecimal number
beginning with a letter (A-F) to be preceded by a zero to
distinguish it from a symbol. This loop delays as long as
possible. (For those of you who want to know exactly how long
this is, it is computed as follows: "DEC HL" requires 6 T
states (basic clock periods), "LD A,H" requires 4, "OR L" 4,
and "JP NZ,LP2" 10. This is a total of 24 T states. The
basic clock frequency of the TRS-80 is 1.77 MHz (563
nanoseconds), so the total time for one occurrence of this
loop is 13512 nanoseconds. 65535 occurrences takes about
.88556 seconds.)

    The outer loop uses the B register, and the decrementing is
done with the DJNZ instruction, which both decrements B and
jumps to the location named LP1 if it is non-zero. While we
are discussing this loop, we should notice that the previous
JP (jump) instruction could be replaced by a JR (jump
relative). This would save one byte of memory used by the
program, although the instruction takes slightly longer to
execute (12 T states instead of 10). In general, it is better
to use jump relatives (when possible) rather than jumps,
because memory is more likely to be the limiting factor than
speed.

    The final instruction in the program, "JP 0", jumps to
location zero, which re-boots TRSDOS or Level II Basic. This

step may not seem important, but it actually is. You must always consider what is supposed to happen when your program is finished, and if you don't know what to do, then you should probably re-boot the system as this program does.

The last line of the program, END, has the symbol START in the operand field. This is the first instruction in the program that is to be executed, which is in line 120. You should always indicate a starting symbol on the END statement, since this will be required when the file is stored on disk or tape. In TRSDOS, you can simply say "RUN PROG" and the program will execute, and when using the SYSTEM command in Level II Basic you can just type "/<ENTER>" and it will run; otherwise, you have to give the starting address in decimal.

Once the program has been typed into the computer, it is time to assemble it. We could use a command like "A PROG/WE" for this purpose. "PROG" is the name of the program that will be written on cassette. (If you have the disk version of EDTASM, you would be asked whether you wanted the program written on cassette or disk here.) "WE" is the "wait on error" option, which is always a good thing to use. The assembler's output will appear as follows:

```
*A PROG/WE
7000              00100           ORG     7000H
3C00              00110 VIDEO     EQU     3C00H
7000  21003C      00120 START     LD      HL,VIDEO      ;SOURCE ADR.
7003  11013C      00130           LD      DE,VIDEO+1    ;DEST. ADDRESS
7006  010004      00140           LD      BC,400H       ;BYTE COUNT
7009  36BF        00150           LD      (HL),0BFH     ;GRAPHICS BYTE
700B  EDB0        00160           LDIR                  ;WRITE OUT SCREEN
                  00170 ;DELAY LOOP TO KEEP WHITED-OUT SCREEN ON
700D  0605        00180           LD      B,5
700F  21FFFF      00190 LP1       LD      HL,0FFFFH     ;VALUE TO DEC
7012  2B          00200 LP2       DEC     HL
7013  7C          00210           LD      A,H
7014  B5          00220           OR      L             ;HL=0?
7015  C21270      00230           JP      NZ,LP2        ;NO? DEC AGAIN
7018  10F5        00240           DJNZ    LP1           ;DEC.B--B=0?
701A  C30000      00250           JP      0H            ;JUMP TO BASIC
7000              00260           END     START
00000   TOTAL ERRORS

LP2       7012        <This is the symbol table>
LP1       700F
VIDEO     3C00
START     7000
READY CASSETTE      <Load cassette tape, set to RECORD>
<ENTER>
*
```

The hexadecimal numbers in the first column on the left show either the value of the location counter when that instruction is being assembled, or the value of the symbol defined or referred to there. The next column, which varies from one to three bytes (two to six characters) in our example, shows the actual machine code. From this point on (in each line), the listing is identical to our source program.   At the end, the assembler tells us how many errors we made, and then prints the symbol table in reverse order of the definition of the symbols.   Finally, the program is recorded on cassette tape. (If we were using disk, this would happen automatically without our having to do anything here.) The "*" at the end is the assembler's prompt for an additional command.

This program is a good introduction to the use of the Editor/Assembler, but it really doesn't do anything useful for us. In the chapters below we will concentrate on more meaningful applications of assembly-language programming.

7
READING AND
PRINTING NUMBERS

Now that we have some understanding of how a program is written in assembly language, and we know how to use the TRS-80 ROM subroutines to read the keyboard and print a character on the video display, we come to the practical subject of writing a program to do something useful. At this point we encounter a number of new complexities that must be reckoned with. Many of the things that we can take for granted when programming in Basic cannot be done so easily in machine language.

Foremost among these is number conversions. When we type in a number at the keyboard -- say an easy number like 1000 -- we are typing a string of decimal digits. The computer receives these one at a time, and has no particular reason for associating them and considering them as one number, unless we tell it how to. Furthermore, the digits that we type are received by the machine in ASCII format. If we want to use the number they represent in computations, we must convert these digits into one hexadecimal value. Once we have done our computations, we will probably want to display any answers that we produce in decimal rather than hexadecimal form; but to print any number requires that we convert the digits to ASCII form and print them one at a time.

Coping with these problems is, in a nutshell, the subject of this chapter. Fortunately, we are not the only people who have ever had to struggle with them, and there are a number of

standard solutions that can be used. Our goal is to be able
to have you get a number into the computer, where you can
operate on it, and back out, where you can see the result.

Let us clarify first that there are many kinds of numbers
employed in a computer. Level II Basic computes with three:
single- and double-precision floating-point numbers,   and
integers.   We will restrict our consideration in this chapter
to integers, specifically those used by Level II, in which the
total amount can be contained in a two-byte word or register
pair (such as BC, DE, or HL).   These numbers have no
fractional values and have a maximum range of -32768 to
+32767, or an absolute value of 0 to 65535.

When we consider a number in a two-byte word, it is stored
in hexadecimal form. All such numbers are actually stored
"backwards" in memory but "correctly" inside any register pair
that contains them. This means that a value like 1023H is
actually stored as 2310 inside memory. This is just a quirk
of the Z-80 that is preserved for compatibility with the 8080
and 8008, and it really makes no difference except if we go
hunting through memory one byte at a time to find a number.

In this chapter, we will consider only three problems:
inputting a hexadecimal number, and printing a number in
hexadecimal or decimal form. These are difficult enough for
beginners. In later chapters we will consider some of the
problems involved in computing with other kinds of numbers.

7.1 Printing a Number in Hexadecimal Form

Suppose that we want to display the hexadecimal value of a
single byte on the video screen. A byte requires exactly two
hexadecimal digits.   We must convert these digits to ASCII
form and print them one at a time. To see what we have to do
here, it is convenient to refer to a chart showing the
relationship between hexadecimal values and ASCII graphics.
Appendix B gives a complete chart of the ASCII values, but we
will reproduce the relevant portions of it here.   In reading
this chart, the numbers at the top show the most-significant
hexadecimal digit and the numbers going down the left side the
least-significant digit.

	2	3	4	5
0	space	0	@	P
1	!	1	A	Q
2	"	2	B	R
3	#	3	C	S
4	$	4	D	T
5	%	5	E	U
6	&	6	F	V
7	'	7	G	W
8	(	8	H	X
9	)	9	I	Y
A	*	:	J	Z
B	+	;	K	up arrow
C	,	<	L	down arrow
D	-	=	M	left arrow
E	.	>	N	right arrow
F	/	?	O	cursor

The 16 possible hexadecimal digits are referred to by the
characters '0' through '9' and 'A' through 'F'. We can see
that these are in two separate portions of the chart and,
fortunately, they are in a logical ascending order.   For
numerical digits, the value of the digit (0-9) plus 30H
produces the ASCII representation. For the letters A-F, we
have to add not 30H, but 37H. The simplest way of producing
an ASCII digit is first to add 30H to the hexadecimal digit,
then test to see whether the result is higher than 39H, and if
so, add 7. Once this is done, we have to perform the same
operation on the other 4-bit hexadecimal digit in the byte.

As we approach this problem, let us consider the machine
operations we will need.   To display the first hexadecimal
digit, we have to move the leftmost 4 bits in the byte (0-3)
over to the rightmost 4 bits (4-7).   This can be done by
either shifting or rotating the byte four times.   There are
many different Z-80 instructions that might be used for this
purpose, but the best ones to use are RRCA or RRA, because
they are faster than some of the others and require only one
byte. RRCA rotates the accumulator right one bit, with the
bit shifted off the end into both the carry and bit 0. The
fact that it is a rotate instruction is irrelevant for our
purpose, but it doesn't matter, because we are going to ignore
bits 0-3 when we are done.

Once the proper value is moved into bits 4-7, we have to
get rid of whatever remains in bits 0-3. An AND instruction
is needed here. AND takes two bytes, one in A and the other
either in another register or in a memory location, and
compares them bit-by-bit. Only if a 1 exists in each of the
two bytes is it kept in the result.   AND 0FH preserves the

rightmost four bits, because 0FH (15) is the hexadecimal equivalent of 00001111 binary, which has ones in the four right bits.

   A complete ASCII display of the hexadecimal value of a byte is accomplished in the subroutine shown below. It is assumed that you have appropriately positioned the cursor on the video display, and that the byte you want to display is in A. DISP calls the ROM subroutine to display a byte (see Chapter 5).

```
;subroutine to print hex value of byte on video display
HEX     PUSH    AF          ;save byte
        RRCA                ;shift
        RRCA                ;bits 0-3
        RRCA                ;into
        RRCA                ;bits 4-7
        CALL    HEX2        ;1st digit
        POP     AF          ;bits 4-7
HEX2    AND     0FH         ;zap 0-3
        ADD     A,30H       ;0 to 9
        CP      3AH         ;if <3A
        JR      C,DISP      ;display
        ADD     A,7         ;A to F
DISP    CALL    33H         ;display
        RET                 ;done
```

   The subroutine ends by falling through to DISP, which returns to the calling program.

   This routine is adequate for displaying a single byte, but what about larger values? For hexadecimal numbers, the solution is easy, because all you have to do is load each byte, one at a time, and call HEX. A subroutine to print the 2-byte value contained in the HL register pair is shown below:

```
;display HL in hex on video display
PHLHEX LD      A,H         ;first H
       CALL    HEX
       LD      A,L         ;then L
       JP      HEX
```

   The jump at the end could be eliminated by physically locating this subroutine immediately before HEX, as we placed HEX before DISP above. Factors like this should always be taken into account when considering where to locate subroutines in memory.

7.2 Printing a Number in Decimal Form

Printing the value of a number in decimal form is a totally
different kind of problem, because there is no convenient
relationship between decimal digits and the bit positions they
occupy. Since a byte can have a value only from Ø to 15,
there is no real necessity to have a routine that displays a
single byte in decimal form; but a routine to display a 2-byte
word in decimal form is quite necessary. As we mentioned
above, a 2-byte word can have a value either from -32768 to
+32767 or from Ø to 65535, depending on whether we consider
the first bit to be a sign. In the following discussion we
will implement the latter method.

In order to display a 2-byte value, we need first to
display the ten-thousands digit, then the thousands, hundreds,
tens, and ones digits. This amounts to five basic steps.
Rather than duplicate the code for each step five times, we
will seek a method that involves one loop that is executed
five times with different data. The basic method is to start
with our number (for example, 28672) and subtract 10ØØØ from
it. If the result is positive (18672), we increment a counter
and subtract 10ØØØ again (yielding 8672). When the result is
finally negative (-1328), we display the value of the counter
(2, the ten-thousands digit) and add back 10ØØØ (8672 again).
Then we start the process over again with 10ØØ, and continue
until we have gone through all five digits.   The following
subroutine implements this process using register IX as a
pointer to the decimal digits, which are contained in a table
called DECTBL:

```
;subroutine to print a 2-byte
;number in decimal form (Ø-65535)
PDEC      LD      IX,DECTBL   ;IX = pointer
PDEC1     XOR     A           ;zero A
          LD      B,(IX+1)    ;BC = decimal
          LD      C,(IX)      ;digit
          OR      A           ;zap carry
PDEC2     SBC     HL,BC       ;subtract BC
          JR      C,PDEC3     ;digit done
          INC     A           ;else increment A
          JR      PDEC2       ;continue
PDEC3     ADD     HL,BC       ;add back
          ADD     A,30H       ;'Ø' to '9'
          CALL    DISP        ;display
          LD      A,C         ;if C=1,
          CP      1           ;done
          RET     Z
          INC     IX          ;else increment
          INC     IX          ;IX twice
          JR      PDEC1       ;digit
```

```
DECTBL   DEFW   10000        ;table
         DEFW   1000
         DEFW   100
         DEFW   10
         DEFW   1
```

   This subroutine assumes that the value to be printed is in
HL when it is called. Note that IX points to the decimal
digits, while BC actually contains their values. A is used
for the counter that is incremented each time the subtraction
yields a positive result. Since we are dealing only with
decimal digits, converting to ASCII requires just adding 30H.
IX must be incremented twice, because each of the values in
the decimal table DECTBL are stored in 2 bytes. This routine
prints leading zeros, and it destroys the previous values of
A, HL, DE, and IX.

7.3   Inputting a Number in Hexadecimal Form

To input hexadecimal digits that represent a single number, we
have a problem similar to what we faced before, but in
reverse. The keyboard reads one digit at a time. This digit
represents a 4-bit quantity inside the number we are creating.
We can either automatically wait to receive four digits, or
more preferably wait for a special character such as ENTER to
signify that the number is finished.

   The following subroutine reads the keyboard and builds a
hexadecimal number in the HL register pair, waiting for ENTER
to terminate the number. If we do not type four digits, zeros
will occupy the unfilled positions; and if we type more than
four, only the last four will be kept. Each digit is
displayed as it is typed.

```
;subroutine to read a hexadecimal
;number from the keyboard into HL
INPUT    LD     HL,0         ;clear HL
INPUT1   CALL   KEYIN        ;get digit
         CP     13           ;ENTER?
         RET    Z            ;if so, done
         CALL   DISP         ;else disp
         CP     '0'          ;if < '0',
         JR     C,INPUT1     ;ignore
         CP     3AH          ;if > '9',
         JR     C,STRIP      ;'0' to '9'
         CP     'A'          ;if < 'A',
         JR     C,INPUT1     ;ignore
         CP     'G'          ;if >= 'G',
         JR     NC,INPUT1    ;ignore
         SUB    7            ;A-F: 3A-3F
```

```
STRIP     AND     15           ;zap bts 0-3
          ADD     HL,HL        ;shift HL
          ADD     HL,HL        ;left 4 bits
          ADD     HL,HL        ;very, very
          ADD     HL,HL        ;slowly
          LD      D,0          ;zero D
          LD      E,A          ;move A to E
          ADD     HL,DE        ;add digit
          JR      INPUT1       ;next digit
KEYIN     CALL    49H          ;ROM keyboard routine
          RET                  ;(see chapter 5)
```

While this subroutine reads and displays any character
typed at the keyboard (except ENTER), the character will be
used only if it is a legitimate hexadecimal digit -- '0' to
'9' or 'A' to 'F'. This is insured by the series of compares
following INPUT1. If the character is an 'A' to 'F', 7 is
subtracted from the ASCII value, thus creating 3A to 3F. Then
the left four bits are masked out (at STRIP). At this point,
the present contents of HL are shifted left four bits, by
being added to themselves four times in succession. This is
an efficient way to do it, and the ADD HL,HL instruction takes
only one byte. Then the number we have inputed, presently
residing in A, is moved to DE; but since it is only one byte,
it is put into E, and D is cleared. Finally, DE is added to
HL, and the subroutine goes to get the next digit. Note that
the previous contents of DE are lost in this process.

7.4   A Sample Program

The following program reads a hexadecimal number from the
keyboard and prints it in decimal form. It is an endless
loop, always looking for a new number after printing the old
one, so you will have to hit RESET to stop it. You can type
gibberish, but the program will accept only legitimate digits.
The number is also displayed in hexadecimal form. You must
hit ENTER after typing the number.

```
          ORG     7000H
START     LD      A,1CH        ;home cursor
          CALL    DISP
          LD      A,1FH        ;clear video
          CALL    DISP
          LD      A,0EH        ;on cursor
          CALL    DISP
NEXT      CALL    INPUT        ;get number
          CALL    SPACE        ;print space
          CALL    PHLHEX       ;hex display
          CALL    SPACE
          CALL    PDEC         ;decimal
```

```
        LD    A,13      ;print CR
        CALL  DISP
        JR    NEXT
SPACE   LD    A,' '
        JR    DISP
;copy PHLHEX here
;copy HEX here
;copy PDEC here
;copy INPUT here
        END   START
```

8

ORGANIZING ARRAYS
AND TABLES

8.1 Arrays

One of the most important principles of writing good programs
is to organize data items so that they can easily be accessed
for whatever purposes they are to be used. This chapter will
be devoted to methods of organizing tables and arrays so that
they can be searched or processed easily by the Z-80.

An ARRAY is the same thing that a SUBSCRIPTED VARIABLE in
Basic is. It is a group of items organized under a single
heading, because the items usually have something in common
that makes it useful to consider them as a group. Arrays may
have several DIMENSIONS. A one-dimensional array is simply a
LIST. A two-dimensional array is usually thought of as being
organized into columns and rows, like a matrix, and a
three-dimensional array is a group of matrices.

When using the TRS-80, there are usually just two kinds of
data that are organized into arrays: ASCII data and numerical
data. ASCII data is the same as STRING data in Basic
programs. There are many different kinds of numerical data:
bytes, integers, BCD numbers, and floating-point numbers are
some of the possibilities. Other types of data that might be
used in some applications include graphics code -- actually
numerical data, but of a very specialized kind -- and actual
machine code.

8.2 ASCII Tables

Data needs to be organized to enable efficient searching through it. The subject of searching is also discussed in connection with the block search instructions in chapter 9. Here, we will go beyond the subject of searching through single bytes to searching through groups of bytes.

Suppose that we have a list of names, and that we want to search through them to find a particular one. Here we might encounter difficulties in distinguishing the beginning and middle of a name. For example, consider the following data:

```
JOSEPH
JOE
JO
```

If we enter these items into a table as they appear above, we see that the letters "JO" appear in each one. One solution is to allocate a certain number of bytes to each item, and pad the rest with blanks. (This is the method used by the Disk Operating System for file names and passwords.) In the following table, all items have a length of eight bytes:

```
DEFM      'JOSEPH  '
DEFM      'JOE     '
DEFM      'JO      '
```

Now if we search for the succession 'JO   ', we will find it only once. But this method is wasteful of memory space, and does not allow for names longer than eight characters. Another solution is to put some special value, such as zero, or 13, the carriage-return character, at the end of each item to signify the end:

```
DEFM      'PHILADELPHIA'
DEFB      0
DEFM      'CHICAGO'
DEFB      0
DEFM      'LOS ANGELES'
DEFB      0
```

This method allows strings of any length to represent an item, but still "wastes" a byte at the end. A similar solution is to put a byte indicating the length of the string at the beginning, following it with the data; but this method also uses an extra byte, and now we would have to count all the letters!

An even better method takes advantage of the fact that ASCII code is only seven bits and does not use the sign bit

(7). Therefore, as long as we remember to eliminate bit 7 when we get the item out of the table, we can set this bit as an indication of the beginning of an item:

```
DEFB     'J'+80H
DEFM     'OSEPH'
DEFB     'H'+80H
DEFM     'ARRY'
DEFB     'T'+80H
DEFM     'HOMAS'
```

This table consists of the names 'JOSEPH', 'HARRY', and 'THOMAS', but the first character has the sign bit set. (This method is used by Level II Basic when it searches for Basic key words.)

You will probably have more frequent occasion to set up tables that consist of more than one list, relating the items in corresponding positions. For example, the following list sets up two data tables, one consisting of the names of items for sale in a supermarket, and the other prices. Items are separated by the carriage return (13), and the end of the table is indicated by a 255 control byte:

	List 1			List 2	
ITEMS	DEFM	'EGGS'	PRICES	DEFM	'.69'
	DEFB	13		DEFB	13
	DEFM	'BREAD'		DEFM	'.79'
	DEFB	13		DEFB	13
	DEFM	'MILK'		DEFM	'.55'
	DEFB	13		DEFB	13
	DEFM	'BUTTER'		DEFM	'1.95'
	DEFB	13		DEFB	13
	DEFB	255		DEFB	255

Note that even though the items in the second list represent prices -- numerical values -- ASCII data is used. This makes it easy to print the values, but more complicated to perform the arithmetic of adding up the bill. If we were going to use this program for that purpose, we would probably replace this data with integer or floating-point numbers.

Now let us consider the problem of writing a program to search through a series of items such as these and to pull out the price of an item selected. The following short program inputs a name and places it into a buffer called QUERY. Since the line input subroutine is used, the item name ends with a carriage return. This is partly the reason we used the CR in the tables above, which are to be copied into the program at the end.

```
; Item - Price Search
        ORG     7000H
START   LD      HL,MSG          ;print 'ITEM?'
PMSG    LD      A,(HL)
        CALL    33H             ;ROM display routine
        INC     HL              ;point to next byte
        CP      '?'             ;did we just print '?'
        JR      NZ,PMSG         ;if not keep going
ITEM    LD      HL,QUERY        ;where to put data
        LD      B,20            ;max length of input
        CALL    40H             ;get line
        JR      C,START         ;if BREAK, try again
        LD      HL,ITEMS        ;HL=>items
        LD      BC,PRICES       ;BC=>prices
ITMLP   LD      DE,QUERY        ;DE=>test string
ITMLP2  LD      A,(DE)          ;1st char of test string
        CP      (HL)            ;compare to 'items' list
        JR      NZ,NOTHIS       ;try next
        CP      13              ;stop at CR in test string
        JR      Z,FOUND         ;eureka!
        INC     DE              ;try next char
        INC     HL              ;of item & query
        JR      ITMLP2          ;repeat
NOTHIS  INC     HL              ;on to next item
        LD      A,(HL)          ;test char
        CP      13              ;CR?
        JR      Z,NEXT          ;yes
        CP      255             ;last item
        JR      NZ,NOTHIS       ;keep trying
        JR      START           ;didn't find - try again
NEXT    INC     HL              ;char after CR
NEXTD   INC     BC              ;now inc price list
        LD      A,(BC)          ;price char
        CP      13              ;CR?
        JR      NZ,NEXTD        ;no
        INC     BC              ;char. after CR
        JR      ITMLP           ;try now
FOUND   LD      A,'$'           ;print '$'
        CALL    33H             ;before price
FOUND2  LD      A,(BC)          ;print price
        CP      13              ;last char?
        JR      Z,START         ;yes
        CALL    33H             ;display
        INC     BC              ;next char
        JR      FOUND2
MSG     DEFB    13              ;print CR before...
        DEFM    'ITEM?'
QUERY   DEFS    20              ;input buffer
ITEMS   DEFM    'EGGS'          ;place ITEMS table here
        ...
PRICES  DEFM    '.69'           ;place PRICES table here
```

```
          ...
          END       START
```

If the subroutine does not find the item after comparing the names, it increments both the item pointer (HL) and the price pointer (DE) and keeps going. The program is an infinite loop, so that it returns and asks you for a new item whether or not it finds the previous item.

The following code could be used instead of that at NOTHIS above:

```
NOTHIS    LD        A,(HL)
          INC       HL
          CP        13
          JR        Z,NEXT
          CP        255
          JR        Z,START
          JR        NOTHIS
NEXT      ...                 ;(NOT INC HL)
```

The difference here is that the "LD A,(HL)" precedes the "INC HL", so that the comparison is always made with the previous value. The first time that this occurs, we already know that A will not be 13 or 255, so the loop is executed one time unnecessarily. However, this eliminates the need for the extra "INC HL" after the loop at NEXT. The same change could be made to eliminate the extra "INC BC" at the end of the next section of code. In writing TRS-80 programs, it is generally preferable to optimize code in favor of using fewer bytes rather than fewer instruction executions, but this is a choice that you must make as a programmer. Here, even if we had thousands of items in the list, the difference in execution time would not be noticeable.

One complicated aspect of the short program above was that it had to keep track of two separate tables. This can be eliminated if the data is organized in a different manner, such as the following:

```
          DEFM      'EGGS$.69'
          DEFB      13
          DEFM      'BREAD$.79'
          DEFB      13
          DEFM      'MILK$.55'
          DEFB      13
          DEFM      'BUTTER$1.95'
          DEFB      255
```

If one table is organized in this manner, the "$" can be used as a separator between one subfield and the other, and it

can also be printed as part of the text. This method would be
valid unless the item names contained imbedded dollar signs --
highly unlikely!

8.3 Command Tables

A problem related to the handling of tables above occurs when
we need to test a series of command letters in order to
perform some action.   If our commands are represented by
single letters, there is no problem, for we can just have a
series of:

```
          CP        'S'
          JP        Z,START
```

But if we have commands of two or more letters, such as 'ST'
for STOP and SW for SWITCH, this type of programming gets very
cumbersome. If HL points to the command word, we could:

```
          CP        'S'
          JR        NZ,NOTS          ;1st char not .S
          INC       HL               ;try next char
          LD        A,(HL)
          CP        'T'
          JP        Z,STOP           ;'ST'
          CP        'W'
          JP        Z,SWITCH         ;'SW'
          DEC       HL               ;restore 1st char
          LD        A,(HL)
NOTS      ...                        ;continue
```

   It is much more efficient to set up a table of command
words and addresses, such as the following:

```
COMTBL    DEFM      'ST'    ;command table
          DEFW      STOP
          DEFM      'SW'
          DEFW      SWITCH
          ...
          DEFB      255
```

   Note the difference between DEFM and DEFW. DEFM defines a
string of ASCII characters, whereas DEFW defines a WORD
containing the address of the memory location defined
elsewhere in the program. 'STOP' and 'SWITCH' are the names
of locations that contain the code executing these functions.

   This table can be searched, so that the program branches to
the correct control word location if a match occurs, as
follows:

```
            LD      HL,(COM)            ;(COM) contains 2-char com
            LD      DE,COMTBL           ;DE=>command table
LOOK        LD      A,(DE)              ;1st letter to A
            INC     DE                  ;point to next letter
            CP      H                   ;compare 1st letters
            JR      NZ,TRYNEX           ;no good
            LD      A,(DE)              ;try second letter
            CP      L
            JR      Z,GOTCHA            ;both match
TRYNEX      INC     DE                  ;2nd letter of command
            INC     DE                  ;2-byte address
            INC     DE
            LD      A,(DE)              ;last entry in table?
            INC     A
            JR      NZ,LOOK             ;no
            JR      DONE                ;yes
GOTCHA      INC     DE                  ;transfer address
            LD      A,(DE)              ;to HL
            LD      L,A                 ;lsb
            INC     DE
            LD      A,(DE)
            LD      H,A                 ;msb
            JP      (HL)                ;execute command
DONE        ...                         ;didn't find anything
```

Note the unusual method that this program uses to test for
the last value in the table. It takes advantage of the use of
the value 255 as the end byte. This value is loaded into A
and A is incremented. If A is now zero, then the previous
value must have been 255 and we are done. This method saves
one byte over the more usual succession:

```
            LD      A,(DE)
            CP      255
```

but the latter method, of course, allows any value to be used
as the end byte.

9

MOVING DATA

In this chapter we will cover one of the most important subjects in TRS-80 assembly language programming: moving data in memory. This is one of the tasks for which the Z-80 microprocessor is ideally suited. Before we get into it, however, there is one thought that you should always keep in mind when writing a program: avoid moving data! Write your programs in such a way that the data is already located where you will need it. Moving data around can consume much execution time, especially if the moves are repeated very often. Lists and tables can be structured so that you don't have to go through each item to find something you are looking for. If you do have to move data, though, at least the programming is simple.

9.1 Moving Blocks

The register pairs BC, DE, and HL, as well as the two index regsters IX and IY, are very important from the standpoint of moving data within the TRS-80, because the address of any memory location can be contained in exactly a two-byte quantity. A BLOCK is any group of contiguous bytes in memory. Suppose that we want to move one block to another. The first block would be called the SOURCE BLOCK and the second the DESTINATION BLOCK. As long as we know the starting address in each block, it is easier to think of the length or byte count of the blocks rather than the ending addresses, because both

blocks are of the same length, even though the ending
addresses are different. To move an entire block of data one
byte at a time, we could load the first byte from the source
block into the accumulator and store it in the destination
block, then decrement the byte counter to see if it is zero.
If not, we increment the pointers to both blocks and continue.
The only problem here is that we cannot test for a zero value
in a double register in just one instruction. Suppose that HL
points to the source block, DE to the destination block, and
BC ("byte count") to the length. The method described above
is implemented in the following program, which moves the
bottom 1K of ROM to the video display (try it!):

```
          ORG     7000H
START     LD      HL,0            ;source block
          LD      DE,3C00H        ;destination = video memory
          LD      BC,400H         ;length = 1K
LOOP      LD      A,(HL)          ;get byte
          LD      (DE),A          ;store in destination block
          DEC     BC              ;decrement length
          LD      A,B             ;BC = 0?
          OR      C
          JR      Z,DONE          ;if zero, done
          INC     HL              ;point to next locations
          INC     DE
          JR      LOOP            ;continue
DONE      CALL    49H             ;wait for keyin
          JP      0               ;re-boot system
          END     START
```

     Only the portion of the program up to DONE is necessary to
move the block. At DONE, the program waits for you to type a
key, then re-boots the system. We will continue to use this
format throughout this chapter.

     This routine requires 12 instructions occupying 20 bytes.
While it works fine, it turns out that everything from LOOP to
the end can be accomplished by just one Z-80 instruction,
LDIR, specifically intended for moving blocks of data.   LDIR
also happens to use the same registers we have used in this
example for the same purposes -- HL points to the source
block, DE to the destination block, and BC to the byte count.
All we have to do is follow the first three instructions above
by LDIR:

```
          ORG     7000H
START     LD      HL,0            ;source block
          LD      DE,3C00H        ;destination block
          LD      BC,400H         ;length
          LDIR                    ;move block
DONE      CALL    49H             ;wait for keyin
```

```
        JP      0                       ;re-boot
        END     START
```

LDIR moves (HL) to (DE) without even affecting the accumulator. This method requires only 11 bytes, and is even faster than the previous loop method.

LDIR is one of the most important Z-80 instructions. It did not exist on the 8080. It is part of a group called the Block Transfer and Search instructions, and there are several similar instructions that should be mentioned in the same context.

LDI also moves blocks of data like LDIR, except that only one byte is moved at a time and the instruction stops. The HL and DE registers are incremented and BC decremented, and the end of the loop is signified by the parity/overflow flag being reset. The reason for using LDI is to stop and do something else after each byte is moved. To continue to move the block, the instruction needs to be included in some kind of loop.

As an example of the use of LDI, suppose that we want to move the first 1K of ROM to the video display as above, but that we want to stop at the first occurrence of the byte 'A'. If this byte is not found, the loop continues until the entire 1K is moved. The following program uses LDI to accomplish this task:

```
        ORG     7000H
START   LD      HL,0            ;source block
        LD      DE,3C00H        ;destination block
        LD      LD,400H         ;length
LOOP    LDI                     ;move one byte
        EX      AF,AF'          ;save flags
        LD      A,(HL)          ;get next byte
        CP      'A'             ;is it 'A'?
        JR      Z,DONE          ;if zero, yes
        EX      AF,AF'          ;restore flags
        JP      PE,LOOP         ;continue on parity even
DONE    CALL    49H             ;wait for keyin
        JP      0               ;re-boot
        END     START
```

The exchange AF with AF' instructions are needed to save the parity/overflow flag while the comparison is made. The compare instruction may reset parity/overflow before the loop is finished. Rather than having the flags saved in memory, they are saved in the alternate register set.

LDD and LDDR are the same as LDI and LDIR, except that the DE and HL registers are decremented rather than incremented

during the operation. Instead of setting HL and DE to the
first location in each block, you start them out at the last
location. CC holds the byte count, as before, and it is
decremented as with LDI and LDIR. These operations are used
when you want to go through the blocks backwards, such as when
searching for something as in our example of LDI above, or
when you want the values of the HL or DE registers to point to
the locations immediately preceding the blocks when finished.
The following example moves the first 1K of ROM to the video
display and looks for the first occurrence of a 'Y' to
terminate the move; but the move is carried out backwards,
starting at the bottom of each block.

```
         ORG     7000H
START    LD      HL,3FFH         ;source block (last address)
         LD      DE,3FFFH        ;destination block
         LD      HL,400H         ;byte count
LOOP     LDD                     ;move one byte
         PUSH    AF              ;save flags in stack
         LD      A,(HL)          ;get next byte
         CP      'Y'             ;is it a 'Y'?
         JR      Z,DONE          ;if zero, yes
         POP     AF              ;retrieve flags
         JP      PE,LOOP         ;continue if parity even
DONE     CALL    49H             ;wait for keyin
         JP      0               ;re-boot
         END     START
```

In this example, the flags are saved in the stack rather than
in the alternate register set.

    It is important to realize that although LDIR and LDDR are
only single instructions, their execution time depends on the
length of the block being moved.   They do not operate
instantaneously; they move one byte at a time. Each move
requires five machine cycles, taking 21 T states or 11.823
microseconds on the TRS-80. Nevertheless, they are among the
most efficient operations of the Z-80.

9.2 Filling Blocks

Filling a block simply involves storing the same value in each
location.   For this purpose, it is easy to employ the first
method illustrated above, where a single register holds the
value and one of the register pairs, particularly HL, points
to the locations in the block. We also need another register
pair such as BC to hold a byte count. We cannot use the
accumulator to hold the value to be stored, because it must be
used repeatedly to test whether BC has been decremented to
zero.   The following example fills the video display with a

completely white graphics block:

```
          ORG     7000H
START     LD      HL,3C00H            ;pointer to video memory
          LD      BC,400H             ;byte count
          LD      D,0BFH              ;graphics block
LOOP      LD      (HL),D              ;store byte
          DEC     BC                  ;decrement count
          LD      A,B                 ;is BC = 0?
          OR      C
          JR      Z,DONE              ;if zero, yes
          INC     HL                  ;point to next location
          JR      LOOP
DONE      CALL    49H                 ;wait for keyin
          END     START
```

It is important to use HL as a memory pointer whenever
possible, because any register can be stored or loaded using
HL, whereas only the accumulator can be used with DE or BC.
(Any register can also be used with the index registers IX and
IY, but these instructions should not be used when moving data
around in this manner, because they take longer and are
intended for different applications.)

While the above method of filling a block is easy enough,
it is also possible to use LDIR or LDDR for the same purpose,
and that method is even easier. The trick is to store the
first byte in the block, and then to set the source address to
the value of this byte and the destination to the byte
immediately following. The byte count is set to one less than
the total length of the block. LDIR then moves the byte
indicated by HL (the first byte, already stored) to the
address indicated by DE (the next location), and the process
continues until the whole block is filled. The following
example also fills the video screen with a graphics block, as
the example above, but uses LDIR to accomplish the task:

```
          ORG     7000H
VIDEO     EQU     3C00H               ;first video location
START     LD      HL,VIDEO            ;first location
          LD      DE,VIDEO+1          ;next location
          LD      BC,3FFH             ;length
          LD      (HL),0BFH           ;store first byte
          LDIR                        ;fill screen
          CALL    49H                 ;wait
          JP      0                   ;re-boot
          END     START
```

This program is identical to the program illustrating the use of the Editor/Assembler program in the User's Manual (Radio Shack catalog number 26-2002).

9.3 Searching Through Blocks

Searching through memory to find a specific value involves the same kind of process as moving a block of data, and the Z-80 also has a special group of search operations analogous to the LDIR group. The most important of these is CPIR. There are also CPI, CPD, and CPDR. CPIR requires that you set HL to the first location of a block and BC to the length. The value to be searched for is loaded into the accumulator. Upon execution of CPIR, each byte in the block is compared with the accumulator. If a match occurs, the instruction is terminated. If not, the search continues until either a match is found or the entire block is searched. If BC is set to zero before the instruction begins, the computer will search through the entire 64K bytes of memory until it finds the value. When the match is found, HL contains the address of the byte following the match, and BC the number of bytes remaining to be searched. In this manner, the search can be continued as soon as the processing of the match is completed. The sign and zero flags are set as a result of the compare, and the parity/overflow flag is reset when BC is finally decremented to zero.

The following example searches through the entire memory of the TRS-80 for the value 253 (FD hexadecimal, the first byte of an IY instruction). When one is found, the address of the location where it is found is displayed (in hexadecimal) and the search continues.

```
VALUE   EQU     ØFDH        ;byte to search for
        ORG     7ØØØH
START   LD      HL,Ø        ;first location to search
        LD      BC,Ø        ;length = 64K
        LD      A,VALUE     ;byte to look for
LOOP    CPIR                ;search
        JP      PO,DONE     ;if PO we're done, else we have match
        EX      AF,AF'      ;save A & flags
        DEC     HL          ;because HL = next loc
        LD      A,H         ;display HL in hex
        CALL    HEX
        LD      A,L
        CALL    HEX
        LD      A,' '       ;print space between addresses
        CALL    33H         ;ROM display routine
        INC     HL          ;restore HL
        EX      AF,AF'      ;get back A & flags
```

```
          JR       LOOP      ;continue
DONE      CALL     49H       ;wait for keyin
          JP       Ø         ;re-boot
;hex display routine - see chapter 7
HEX       PUSH     AF
          RRCA
          RRCA
          RRCA
          RRCA
          CALL     HEX2
          POP      AF
HEX2      AND      15
          ADD      A,3ØH
          JR       C,DISP
          ADD      A,7
DISP      CALL     33H
          RET
          END      START
```

   To have the program search for another value, simply change
the argument field in the VALUE EQU statement. If you want to
see something amusing, change it to 255 and see what happens!
(If you want to know why this happens, just remember that 255
is the value that you get in locations where no memory
actually exists.)

   The other search operations CPI, CPD, and CPDR are
analogous to LDI, LDD, and LDDR. CPI and CPD search only one
byte at a time and stop, and CPD and CPDR search backwards
through memory. While we will not demonstrate their use here,
you can probably imagine situations where they might be
preferable to CPIR.   In any event, it is easy to see the
usefulness of these operations.

10
ARITHMETIC OPERATIONS WITH INTEGERS

One of the most important limitations of all 8-bit microprocessors is their ability to perform only a few arithmetic operations. The Z-80 instruction set includes only the operations of addition and subtraction of 8- and 16-bit numbers. (The Z-80 is an improvement over the 8080, which does not include a 16-bit subtract operation!) This means that almost all computation -- not only multiplication and division, but also addition and subtraction of larger quantities -- must be carried out in rather complicated subroutines which perform repeated additions and subtractions.

The question of the form in which the numbers are represented in memory is thus of crucial importance. For the TRS-80, there are really only two sets of number formats to consider: those provided in the Z-80 instruction set, and those in Level II Basic. Other formats can be implemented for various reasons, such as to achieve greater precision.

10.1 8-Bit Addition

The basic 8-bit arithmetic operations require the use of
the accumulator to hold one of the operands and the result of
the operation. The operations are as follows:

```
ADD    A,r        Adds the contents of register r to A.
ADD    A,(HL)     Adds the contents of the location
                  whose address is in HL to A.
ADD    A,n        Adds the value n to A.
ADD    A,(IR+d)   Adds the contents of the location
                  (IX+d)  or  (IY+d) to A.
```

The condition codes are set to reflect the results of the
operations. If zero is produced, the Z flag is set. The sign
flag is copied from the sign bit of the accumulator.

What happens if the result produced is too large to be
contained in the accumulator? Let us clarify this situation
through an example.   If we add the two largest possible
numbers together, 255 + 255 = 510, we find that 510 is too
large to be contained in a single byte. Any result that can
be obtained through the addition of two bytes requires at most
one extra BIT, and what the Z-80 does is to put this bit into
the carry flag. The P/V flag is also set to indicate an
overflow (which would be detected through the use of the PO
condition, because this is the same as odd parity).   This
operation can be illustrated as follows:

register	binary	hexadecimal	decimal
A	1111 1111	FF	255
B	1111 1111	FF	255
Carry 1 A	1111 1110	FE	254

Since the carry bit occupies the position of the ninth bit,
its value is 256, which, when added to 254, gives the correct
result of 510.

This extra bit of precision can now be used in subsequent
operations, to propagate the correct result into other bytes,
which, when grouped with the original byte, are large enough
to hold the correct result. To carry out this propagation,
there is another set of operations that add or subtract the
carry bit along with the two bytes. These operations are as
follows:

```
ADC    A,r          Adds A + r + carry
ADC    A,(HL)       Adds A + (HL) + carry
ADC    A,n          Adds A + n + carry
ADC    A,(IR+d)     Adds A + (IX+d) + carry
                    or A + (IY+d) + carry
```

Some of the applications of these operations are illustrated below in the multiple-precision operations.

10.2 Negative Numbers; Two's-Complement Notation

Thus far, we have been discussing the values contained in bytes as if they all represented positive or absolute values. In fact, they often represent negative values, and the Z-80 has a special way of indicating negative numbers. As we discuss this subject, it is important to keep in mind that several bytes are often grouped together to contain large values, and in this case only one sign applies to the entire group of bytes.

First, negative numbers are represented by considering bit 7, the leftmost bit, to be a SIGN. 0 indicates a positive number and 1 a negative number. Only 7 bits are then left to hold the value of the number. Second, negative numbers are represented in a form called TWO'S-COMPLEMENT NOTATION.

If the sign of a byte is positive, the 7 bits of data simply indicate the value of the number, which can thus range from (+) 0 to 127. For example, if the bits in a byte read 0011 0010, the value is 32 hexadecimal which equals 50 decimal. You might think that if you changed the sign bit to 1 the number would represent -50, but in fact this is not the way that two's-complement notation works. To understand two's complement, you must first understand the ONE'S COMPLEMENT. The one's complement of a binary number is formed by changing all the zeros to ones and ones to zeros. This is easy. In our example, the one's complement of 0011 0010 is 1100 1101. To form the two's complement, you add 1 to the one's complement. The two's complement of 0011 0010 is thus 1100 1111   Let us illustrate this process in a couple of examples:

(a) Find the two's complement of +96 (60 hexadecimal):

hexadecimal	binary	
60	0110 0000	given number
9F	1001 1111	one's complement
	+ 1	add 1
A0	1010 0000	two's complement

(b) Find the two's complement of +127 (7F hexadecimal):

hexadecimal	binary	
7F	0111 1111	given number
80	1000 0000	one's complement
	+ 1	
81	1000 0001	two's complement

The curious thing about two's-complement notation is that the value of MINUS ZERO does not exist. Instead, -128 does. The complete range of signed values for bytes is thus -128 to +127.

Since negative numbers are so important, the Z-80 has a separate instruction, NEG, that produces the negative equivalent of a byte. There is also a CPL instruction that produces the one's complement. (CPL exists on the 8080, but NEG does not.)

Why do computers use two's-complement notation? The reason is that it simplifies the operation of arithmetic computations. Any combination of additions and subtractions will work. When two's-complement notation is used, the sum of a number and its negative value is always 256, which comes out to be zero when the extra bit shifts into the carry. Thus, whether bytes represent values of -128 to +127 or 0 to 255 is entirely a way of interpreting the number. Sometimes you can decide to use the sign and other times not to.

10.3 8-Bit Subtraction

Now that we understand negative numbers, let us consider the 8-bit subtraction operations. They parallel exactly the 8-bit addition operations:

```
SUB    r          Subtracts the contents of r from A.
SUB    (HL)       Subtracts the value in (HL) from A.
SUB    n          Subtracts n from A.
SUB    (IR+d)     Subtracts the value in (IX+d) or
                  (IY+d) from A.
SBC    A,r        Subtracts r and the carry bit from A.
SBC    A,(HL)     A - (HL) - carry
SBC    A,n        A - n - carry
SBC    A,(IR+D)   A - (IX+d) - carry or
                  A - (IY+d) - carry
```

Why is A indicated as an operand with SBC and not with SUB? The rule is that A must be indicated as the first operand whenever there is another possible Z-80 instruction that uses another first operand. In this example, "SBC HL,DE" is a

possible operation, but "SUB HL,DE" is not.   There is a 16-bit
SBC operation, but no 16-bit SUB operation.   Another point to
note is that, when dealing with   subtract   operations,   it   is
more   relevant   to think of the carry bit as a "borrow" rather
than as a carry, but the letter C is what is indicated in   the
mnemonic.

    If we consider some examples of subtraction operations,   we
can see the way that the two's-complement notation works:

(a)   Subtract 20 from 8 (8 - 20 = -12)

    The   easiest   way   to   explain   the   functioning   of   this
operation is to do it the same way that you would if you   were
doing   the   arithmetic   by   hand: note that -20 is of greater
magnitude than 8, and therefore subtract 8 from 20 and   negate
the answer:

hexadecimal	binary	decimal
14	0001 0100	20
08	0000 1000	8
---------	---------	
0C	0000 1100	12
F3	1111 0011	one's complement
	+ 1	
F4	1111 0010	-12

(b)   Add 8 and -20 (8 + (-20) = 12)

08	0000 1000	8
EA	1110 1010	-20
---------	---------	
F4	1111 0010	-12

    This example was included to verify that the addition of   a
negative number would also produce the correct result.

(c)   Add 234 and 8

08	0000 1000	8
EA	1110 1010	234
---------	---------	
F4	1111 0010	242

    This   example   shows   that   the   Z-80   is indifferent as to
whether the   bytes   added   are   considered   positive   unsigned
numbers   or signed numbers.   The results are correct in either
case.   To   verify   that   the   binary   answer   is   correct,   we
evaluate   each of the bits as follows: 2 + 16 + 32 + 64 + 128
= 242.

When a subtract with carry operation occurs, it subtracts not only the number, but also the carry bit. Thus, while an ADC operation may make the result 1 greater because of the carry bit, an SBC operation may make it 1 less.

10.4 Multiple-Precision Addition and Subtraction

The 8-bit addition and subtraction operations can be combined to perform calculations on any size quantities. As an example of this sort of operation, we will first use the 8-bit operations to perform 16-bit calculations. These can then be compared to and verified by the 16-bit operations. The following routine adds two two-byte values whose addresses are contained in the IX and IY registers. For compatibility with 16-bit operations, it is assumed that the bytes are stored "backwards" in memory (least-significant byte first):

```
LD      A,(IX)       ;get lsb of 1st value
ADD     A,(IY)       ;add lsb of 2nd value
LD      (IX),A       ;save in (IX)
LD      A,(IX+1)     ;get msb of 1st value
ADC     A,(IY+1)     ;now add the carry too
LD      (IX+1),A     ;store in (IX+1)
```

The main point illustrated by this example is that the carry bit must be added the second time but not the first. Also, while this example takes six instructions, it is not particularly difficult, and four of the six instructions are used to retrieve and store the data.

The following subroutine performs a 16-bit subtraction operation, subtracting the value in the DE register pair from that in HL and storing the result in HL. It is equivalent to the Z-80 operation "SBC HL,DE", but has a very practical application to the 8080 microprocessor, since the 8080 does not include this instruction:

```
DSBC    PUSH    AF       ;save previous value of AF
        LD      A,L      ;get lsb of 1st operand
        SUB     E        ;subtract lsb
        LD      L,A      ;save in·L
        LD      A,H      ;get msb
        SBC     D        ;subtract msb
        LD      H,A      ;save in H
        POP     AF       ;restore AF
        RET              ;return
```

We can verify that the result produced by this subroutine is identical to that produced by the SBC HL,DE instruction by

comparing   the   results   later.   (There   is   one difference,
however: the condition codes are not the same.)

It is now easy to see how these operations can be extended
to greater precision through the use of   additional   bytes   to
hold   the   numbers.   The following subroutine performs a 4-byte
integer addition to two sequences of bytes whose addresses are
held   in   the   HL and DE register pairs, the former also being
used to hold the result.   4-byte   integers   like   these   are
capable   of   containing   values   up to 2 to the 31st power -1,
which equals 2,147,483,647.   In this case the   bytes   are   all
stored   backwards   in   memory,   so that when the subroutine is
entered the registers point to the least-significant bytes:

```
ADD4      LD      A,(DE)    ;get lsb of first number
          ADD     A,(HL)    ;add lsb of second number
          LD      (HL),A    ;save
          LD      B,3       ;3 remaining bytes
ADD4LP    INC     HL        ;point to next bytes
          INC     DE
          LD      A,(DE)    ;get next byte
          ADC     A,(HL)    ;add the carry this time
          LD      (HL),A    ;save
          DJNZ    ADD4LP    ;continue
          RET               ;done
```

Since the addition of all bytes after the first can be done
in a loop, the code for this routine is not significantly more
complicated than a 16-bit add loop.   In   fact,   as   the   next
example   shows,   all   operations   can be done in a single loop
through the use of an additional instruction: OR A, which has
the   sole   effect   of clearing the carry bit, without changing
the value in the accumulator.   If the carry is cleared   before
the   first   instruction   is   executed,   but   not   after   the
subsequent ones, the add or subtract with carry operations can
be   used   exclusively.   The following subroutine does a 4-byte
subtraction   corresponding   exactly   to   the   4-byte   addition
above,   using   only   the   SBC   operation,   so   that   the whole
subroutine is one loop.   The HL and DE registers are   used   to
hold   the   addresses   of   the operands, DE holding that of the
minuend and HL the subtrahend:

```
SUB4      LD      B,4       ;4-byte subtract
          OR      A         ;clear carry
SUB4LP    LD      A,(DE)    ;get minuend
          SBC     A,(HL)    ;subtract subtrahend
          LD      (DE),A    ;save difference
          INC     DE        ;point to next bytes
          INC     HL
          DJNZ    SUB4LP    ;continue
          RET               ;done
```

10.5 Compare Operations

Compare operations are equivalent to subtracts, only with one important difference: the values in the registers are unchanged.   Only the condition codes are affected.   The Z-80 has only 8-bit compare operations, all of which require using the accumulator.   The most obvious application of compares is to test whether the value in the accumulator is equal to some other number, but it is also possible to test whether it is greater or less than another value. Compare instructions are almost always followed immediately by conditional JP or JR instuctions.   Thus, it is most useful to remember the meanings of the various conditions:

condition	means that...
Z	the value compared was EQUAL to that in the accumulator.
NZ	the two values are UNEQUAL.
C	the absolute value in A is LESS THAN the compared value.
NC	the absolute value of A is GREATER THAN OR EQUAL TO the compared value.
M	The signed value of A is LESS THAN the compared value.
P	The signed value of A is GREATER THAN OR EQUAL TO the compared value.
PO	An overflow was produced by the compare operation.
PE	No overflow was produced by the compare operation.

The Z and NZ conditions present no problem, while the difference between C and M on the one hand, and NC and P on the other, require additional explanation. Use of the P and M conditions, which could be renamed NS ("no sign" = P) and S ("sign" = M) by analogy with the others, depends on whether you are using numbers in the positive and negative sense and evaluating bytes on a -128 to +127 basis. -2 is less than +1, but the absolute value is greater because -2 is FE hexadecimal in two's-complement form, whereas +1 is 01. The sign bit is a copy of bit 7 of the accumulator.

The C and NC conditions do not depend on the sign, but rather on the absolute value of the bytes, on a scale from 0 to 255.   If the value of -1 in the accumulator is compared with +1, the NC condition will be set, because the absolute value of -1 is FF = 255. The advantage of using C and NC is that the jump relative instructions recognize these conditions (as well as Z and NZ), but not P and M (nor PO and PE).

10.6 16-Bit Instructions

As we mentioned above, the Z-80 also has 16-bit addition and subtraction operations. Most of these use the HL register pair in the same way that the 8-bit operations use the accumulator. The index registers can also be used for addition only. The operations are as follows:

```
ADD     HL,ss        ss must be BC, DE, HL, or SP
ADC     HL,ss
SBC     HL,ss
ADD     IR,pp        pp must be BC, DE, SP, IX,
                     or IY (IX can be added only
                     to IX and IY to IY)
```

One of the first important differences between the 8-bit and 16-bit operations is that the 16-bit operations require that the operands reside in the registers themselves. No add or subtract with memory or immediate data exists. Fortunately, the Z-80 also has instructions that load double registers directly to or from memory (the 8080 only allowed this with HL).

There are two important applications of the 16-bit operations: the computation of memory addresses and integer arithmetic in Level II Basic. Any memory address can be contained in a 16-bit register. You can thus compute the addresses where data are stored if you need to. Level II Basic integers may have values from -32768 to +32767. The main difference between these two applications is the same as between signed and absolute bytes: memory addresses are usually considered on an absolute scale from 0 to 65535, while Level II Basic integers use the sign bit. If you are familiar with the PEEK and POKE statements, perhaps you already know that if you want to PEEK or POKE from locations 32760 to 32770, you have to go from 32760 to 32767, and then from -32768 to -32766. The rule for this anomaly is that if the PEEK or POKE address is above 32767, you must subtract it from 65536. Locations 32768 to 65535 are thus referred to by -32768 to -1.

The 16-bit instructions can be used to perform the same multiple-precision adds and subtracts mentioned above, in fewer instructions. The problem here is that the register pairs cannot be used to contain addresses, since they have to be used to hold the data itself. This requires either reorganizing the use of the registers in the subroutines, or using additional instructions to fetch and store the bytes. The following subroutine performs a 32-bit add as shown above, using the 16-bit instructions. In this example, IX and IY contain the addresses of the first byte of the operands.

IX is also used as a pointer to the result.

```
ADD4    LD      B,2                 ;loop twice
        OR      A                   ;clear carry
ADD4LP  LD      L,(IX)              ;1st byte of 1st operand
        LD      H,(IX+1)            ;2nd byte of 1st operand
        LD      E,(IY)              ;1st byte of 2nd operand
        LD      D,(IY+1)            ;2nd byte of 2nd operand
        ADC     HL,DE               ;perform addition
        LD      (IX),L              ;save lsb
        LD      (IX+1),H            ;save msb
        INC     IX                  ;inc each reg twice
        INC     IX                  ;since 2 bytes
        INC     IY                  ;added each time
        INC     IY
        DJNZ    ADD4LP              ;continue
        RET                         ;done
```

It can easily be seen that the additional work required to fetch and store the data makes this method unwieldy and cumbersome. Note also that the previous contents of HL, DE, and B are lost in the above subroutine. Saving and restoring them would require a minimum of six additional instructions.

The main advantage of the 16-bit arithmetic instructions is that they can be built right into the code of a program section, so that they do not require calling an external subroutine, which is necessary for most other types of arithmetic performed by the Z-80.

One final note. All 16-bit numbers, whether they represent addresses in machine instructions or Level II Basic integers, are stored "backwards" in memory, with the least-significant byte first. This is done automatically by the LD instructions, so that you never have to worry about it, except if you go PEEKing through the individual bytes in memory. As we have seen, one advantage of this method (which goes back to the 8008, the predecessor of the 8080) is that the bytes can be added in the order in which they occur in memory, for multiple-precision operations.

10.7 INC and DEC

The INC ("increment") and DEC ("decrement") operations are also classified as arithmetic operations, because they add or subtract 1 from the registers, even though the value 1 can never be changed. There is a fundamental distinction between the single- and double-register INC and DEC instructions. INC r and DEC r affect the condition codes, but INC ss and DEC ss do not. Unfortunately, Zilog uses the same mnemonic in each

case, so the only way to keep it straight is to note carefully
the operands. (In Intel's 8080 mnemonics, "INC ss" and "DEC
ss" are replaced by "INX s" and "DCX s". "X" is always used
for double registers, and "s" is the first register of the
pair.)

INC and DEC should always be used when you want to add or
subtract only one from a register, because the operation
requires only one byte and executes in 4 T cycles. These are
also convenient when you need to step through a series of
bytes one-at-a-time, as we saw above in the multiple-precision
addition and subtraction loops.

Single registers can be used to hold a count of the number
of times a series of instructions is to be executed. This
feature is provided automatically in the DJNZ instruction,
which DECrements B and branches to a nearby location if B is
non-zero (it is a jump relative). Up to 256 iterations can be
achieved by this method, because the register is decremented
before the "JR NZ" occurs (to get 256 iterations, start B with
the value zero). Similar operations can be carried out using
any single register, although two instructions (the DEC and JR
or JP NZ) are needed.

A similar procedure can be instituted with the double
registers, but the fact that these INCs and DECs do not affect
the condition codes forces a revision in the procedure. The
use of two registers makes it possible to go through up to
65536 iterations in a loop. A special process is necessary to
test whether the value in the double register is zero. One of
the most common methods of doing this is the following, which
tests whether HL is zero:

```
        LD      A,H     ;load A from H
        OR      L       ;or A with L
        JR      NZ,LOC  ;if non-zero, continue
```

(Why this works will be explained later in our discussion of
logical operations.) The disadvantage of this method is that
it destroys the value in the accumulator, but practically any
other method would either do the same or would be more complex
than simply saving and restoring A.

11

FLOATING-POINT AND BCD NUMBERS

11.1   Floating-Point Numbers

FLOATING-POINT NUMBERS are the most common method by which
numbers containing both an integer portion and a fractional
portion are represented in computers. A floating-point number
contains a SIGN, EXPONENT, and FRACTION. There is also a sign
of the exponent. The Level II Basic Reference Manual claims
that the fraction contains a certain number of SIGNIFICANT
FIGURES. Actually, it contains a number of significant BITS,
which more or less correspond to a number of significant
decimal digits. The only difference between single- and
double-precision numbers is the number of bytes used for the
fraction. Single-precision numbers use three, and double-
precision seven.   The exponent is the same in each case and
requires one byte. The accuracy of double-precision numbers
is greater, but still not perfect, as we will see below.

Floating-point numbers on the TRS-80 have the following
format: the last byte contains the exponent, and the order of
the first three bytes is "backwards" in memory. The last byte
is what you will see if you PRINT PEEK(VARPTR(X)+3) for
single-precision numbers, where X is the number, or
PEEK(VARPTR(X)+7) for double precision numbers. The first bit
represents the sign of the exponent, 1 being used for positive
exponents and Ø for negative exponents. A "positive" exponent
means that the binary point (same as "decimal point" but for
binary numbers) is moved to the right, and a "negative"

94

exponent means that it is moved to the left, producing a value less than 1. The exponent itself is contained in the remaining seven bits, and thus can range from -127 to +127. There is one exception: if this whole byte is zero, then the number itself is zero. 2 to the 127th power allows a range of values up to about 10 to the 37th or 10 to the -39th power. Any number in this range is represented with about six significant figures for single-precision numbers, or 16 significant figures for double-precision numbers. The following are some examples of floating-point exponents:

hexadecimal	binary	meaning
81	1000 0001	+1: point moved one bit to the right
83	1000 0011	+3: point moved 3 bits to the right
7D	0111 1101	-3: point moved 3 bits to the left
80	1000 0000	+0: the point is immediately to the left of the first bit

The fraction of the number gives its value and is contained in the remaining bytes in a backwards order. In addition, the first byte of the fraction, stored next to last in memory (VARPTR(X)+2 for single-precision numbers), gives the SIGN of the number in its leftmost bit, 0 indicating a positive and 1 a negative number. There is no difference between positive and negative numbers except for this bit (no two's-complement notation for floating-point numbers!). This leaves the most-significant bit unaccounted for, and THIS BIT IS ALWAYS IMPLIED TO BE A 1. A fraction consisting of 3 bytes of zeros thus actually represents +1 binary. Now all we have to do to evaluate floating-point numbers is to remember that each binary bit represents a power of 2. Positive values equal 1, 2, 4, 8, 16, etc., and negative values 1/2, 1/4, 1/8, 1/16, etc. The following examples illustrate how some floating-point values are actually stored in memory:

hexadecimal (order in memory)	binary fraction (correct order)	decimal value
(a) 00 00 00 81	1000 0000 0000 0000 0000 0000	1.0

The binary value of this number is 1 followed by all zeros. The exponent +1 means that the binary point is moved one bit to the right, producing 1.0000 (etc.). The sign of the number is positive.

(b)   00 00 40 83   1100 0000 0000 0000 0000 0000   6.0

When the exponent of +3 is applied, the binary number produced
is 110.0, which equals decimal 6.

(c)   00 00 40 81   1100 0000 0000 0000 0000 0000   1.5

Moving the exponent one bit to the right produces 1.1 binary.
".1" represents one-half in binary notation, so this number is
1.5.

(d)   00 00 F0 84   1111 0000 0000 0000 0000 0000   -15.0

1111 binary equals 15, but don't forget that the first bit of
the third byte is the sign of the number.

(e)   00 00 F0 80   1111 0000 0000 0000 0000 0000   0.9375

The exponent 0 means that the binary point is immediately to
the left of .1111. This value is thus 1/2 + 1/4 + 1/8 + 1/16
=0.9375. This example shows that, for values less than one,
you don't always have exactly six significant figures. Here
is a four-digit number represented completely correctly in
only four bits. Most numbers do not have such accuracy.

(f)   CD CC 4C 7D   1100 1100 1100 1100 1100 1101   0.1

Just looking at the binary value of this number tells you that
it is a repeating fraction in binary form, just as 1/3 in
decimal form gives .33333.... The exponent 7D equals -3, so
the fraction is .00011001100 etc. The value is computed as
1/16 + 1/32 + 1/256 + 1/512 etc. = .0625 + .03125 + .00390625
+ .001953125 = .099609375, getting closer and closer to .1 as
the process continues.

     These examples illustrate some of the problems that occur
when using floating-point numbers.   Many decimal numbers
cannot be represented precisely without losing some tiny bit
of accuracy. When many arithmetic operations are performed on
the same values, the magnitude of this inaccuracy increases.
This   imprecision is a result of the method of number
representation, and does not disappear when double-precision
numbers are used, although the amount of error decreases. You
must remember that the number always contains significant
figures (bits).   If you add 100000.0 and .0001 using single-
precision numbers, the result will be 100000 because of the
loss of significance past the sixth digit. Figuring out the
value represented by some number, or figuring the
floating-point number corresponding to some value, is no easy
task.

What these examples illustrate is that it is difficult enough to understand just how floating-point numbers are represented inside the computer, let alone how to do arithmetic on them. Each arithmetic operation requires a complicated subroutine that may execute thousands of machine instructions for each call. While Basic may be slow in general, it is usually preferable to perform such operations as floating-point calculations using Basic rather than assembly language.

11.2   Binary-Coded-Decimal Numbers

There is another number format frequently used with the 8080 and Z-80 microprocessors. It was considered to be so important by the designers of these microprocessors that they included a special machine operation and two special flags to enable arithmetic operations to be done easily in this form. This number format is called BINARY-CODED-DECIMAL or BCD. The special operation is the DAA ("decimal adjust accumulator") instruction, and the flags are the half-carry (H) and Add/Subtract (N) flags, which are used only by DAA, although they are set or reset by many operations.

The advantages of BCD numbers are that they are inherently very easy to understand, and any inaccuracies they contain are the same for decimal numbers with which we are so familiar. Although four bits can contain values from 0 to 15, the values from 10 to 15 are never used. Instead, when a DAA operation is performed, any values above 9 are adjusted, so that the maximum value contained in a digit is 9 and in a byte 99, the excess value being shifted into the carry bit.

Any series of N BCD bytes contains N x 2 decimal digits. In our examples below, we will restrict our use of decimal numbers to two-byte quantities capable of holding values from 0 to 9999. We will first illustrate some BCD numbers, and then arithmetic operations (addition and subtraction) performed on them. One convenient property of BCD numbers is that their decimal and hexadecimal values are the same.

```
(a)     decimal:        1    2    3    4
        binary:      0001 0010 0011 0100

(b)     decimal:        5    6    7    8
        binary:      0101 0110 0111 1000

(c)     decimal:        9    9    9    9     (maximum
        binary:      1001 1001 1001 1001    value)
```

When arithmetic operations are performed on BCD numbers, we have to remember that there are no special operations that are different from binary additions and subtractions, but BCD numbers must be adjusted so that they never represent a value of more than 9 in any digit. This is where the special DAA operation is required.   How it works may be seen from some examples:

```
(d)     decimal              binary
          1234               0001 0010 0011 0100
        + 5555               0101 0101 0101 0101
          6789               0110 0111 1000 1001
        hexadecimal =>        6    7    8    9
```

Since the sum of any two digits is not greater than 9, no adjustment was needed here.

```
(e)     decimal              binary
          6789               0110 0111 1000 1001
        + 1111               0001 0001 0001 0001
          7900               0111 1000 1001 1010
        hexadecimal =>        7    8    9    A        wrong!
```

When the sum of two digits is greater than 9, a correction in the form of a carry is required, just as it is when you add two digits by hand. The important and simple fact about this carry is that the computer can do it just by looking at each successive digit, starting with the least-significant one. This adjustment is made by means of the DAA instruction.   If the value in any 4-bit digit after an add operation is performed is greater than 9, 6 is added to it and a carry is added to the next digit.   The right digit within the byte sends its carry to the left digit, and the left digit sends it to the next byte by means of the carry flag. If the result is greater than 9999, it cannot be contained within two bytes anyway, so it languishes in the carry bit, and the result shows only the right four digits. As long as DAA is performed after each operation, the result will never get off.

In example (e) above, if a DAA is performed after the first (rightmost) addition which yielded 9A, A would be changed to 0 and 1 added to 9, producing another 0 and setting the carry bit. When the carry is added to the next byte it produces 79, thus yielding the correct value of 7900 as the result.

```
(f)     decimal              binary
          9999               1001 1001 1001 1001
        + 1111               0001 0001 0001 0001
         11110                A    A    A    A
        DAA by +6:           1    1    1    1        carry: 1
```

Here we see that, after we perform the DAA operation, the
result is 1110, which is correct except that the first digit
is missing, but the carry bit is set.

Writing a subroutine to perform BCD addition is really
quite simple. The following subroutine uses index register IX
as a pointer to the first operand and IY for the second. The
result is stored in IX. The number of bytes in the BCD number
is set to 2 by the LD B,2 instruction, but could be set to a
larger value by simply changing this number.

```
BCDADD   OR      A          ;clear carry
         LD      B,2        ;2-digit add
ADDLP    LD      A,(IX)     ;get first operand
         ADC     A,(IY)     ;add second operand
         DAA                ;adjust result
         LD      (IX),A     ;store result
         INC     IX         ;point to
         INC     IY         ;next bytes
         DJNZ    ADDLP      ;continue till done
```

This subroutine clears the carry bit at the beginning so that
it can do all the additions in one loop using ADC.

(g)	decimal	binary			
	5432	0101	0100	0011	0010
	-1928	0001	1001	0010	1000
	3504	0011	1011	0000	1010
	hexadecimal =>	3	B	0	A	wrong!
	DAA by -6:	3	5	0	4	right

How does the Z-80 know whether the last operation was an
add or subtract, meaning that the DAA has to adjust the result
by +6 or -6? The answer is that the N flag is set only by
subtract operations and reset by add operations. Similarly,
the half-carry flag is set only if the right 4 bits are
greater than 9. The H flag is like an "internal" carry, since
its only function is to adjust the left digit.

These examples show that BCD arithmetic is easy to
understand. Other advantages are the simplicity of converting
numbers for printing them, which requires only a hexadecimal
print routine, and the ability to insert a decimal point
between any two digits in a series of bytes, for fractional
arithmetic.

Surprisingly, BCD arithmetic is not used by the TRS-80 for
Level II Basic or any of the standard Radio Shack software.
It thus remains one of the most underutilized resources of the
TRS-80.

12

LOGICAL AND BIT OPERATIONS

12.1 Logical Operations

There is another category of computer operations that are not as widely known as arithmetic operations. These are LOGICAL OPERATIONS. They all operate on the individual bits of the byte in the accumulator, which is compared to another byte specified as the operand. There are three operations executed by the Z-80: AND, OR, and XOR (exclusive OR). An AND operation produces a 1 bit in the result only if both the corresponding bits in the accumulator AND the operand are 1. OR produces a 1 if the bit in either the first operand OR the second operand, OR BOTH, are 1. XOR produces a 1 if either the bit in the first operand or the second operand, BUT NOT BOTH, are 1. These are summarized in the following table:

	binary	hexadecimal
accumulator	0000 1111	0 F
operand	0011 0011	3 3
	---------	---
result of AND	0000 0011	0 3
result of OR	0011 1111	3 F
result of XOR	0011 1100	3 C

The carry bit is ALWAYS cleared (set to zero) by the logical operations. Logical operations never produce ones in bits unless they are already present in the operands. Their functions are to "combine" bits in various ways.

The logical operations have several applications for which they are customarily used. AND is used to MASK OUT certain bits in a byte. A zero in the operand byte masks out a bit, and a one preserves it, if present. For example, in printing hexadecimal numbers, it is necessary to print the value corresponding to each 4-bit digit. If we want to print the least-significant digit, we need to mask out the left four bits. This could be done by an AND 0FH or AND 15 instruction. (When "H" is appended to numbers, it indicates that they are hexadecimal.) Hexadecimal values are frequently specified as operands to logical operations because it is possible to translate them directly into bits.

OR is used to "combine" the values of two bytes into one. For example, to print the value of a digit from 0 to 9, it is necessary first to discover the value to be printed, and then to convert it to ASCII form. The ASCII representations of the digits 0 to 9 are 30H to 39H. It is thus necessary to put the value 0 to 9 into the right four bits, and a "3" into the left four bits. Assuming that the right four bits contain a 0 to 9, the "3" can be combined with the others by an OR 30H operation.

Another use of OR is to clear the carry bit. The operation OR A, which ORs the accumulator with itself, changes no bit values in the accumulator, but resets the carry. AND A also works for this purpose. These are more efficient than any other method, because the instructions take only one byte and 4 T cycles.

Another use of the OR operation occurs when testing the value in a double register for zero. The sequence of operations:

```
    LD      A,H
    OR      L
```

will produce a zero in A only if the values in both H and L are zero.

One of the most frequent applications of XOR is to zero the accumulator, which is done by the XOR A operation. This also clears the carry bit. Other uses of XOR are somewhat more complicated than the other logical operations. For example, it is possible to set up a "toggle switch" using the accumulator and an XOR operation. If A is set to 1 or 0, each time an XOR 1 operation is executed, the value in A will alternate between 1 and 0. This type of alteration is possible only between two values.

Another such application on the TRS-80 occurs with the

blinking asterisks that appear in the upper right corner of
the video display when cassette tapes are read. The ASCII
value of the asterisk is 2AH, and that of the blank space is
20H. The address of the upper right corner is 3C3FH. The
following sequence of operations will cause the character in
the right corner of the screen to change to the opposite
value, alternating between an asterisk and a blank:

```
        LD      A,(3C3FH)       ;get character
        XOR     10              ;2AH - 20H = 10
        LD      (3C3FH),A       ;replace new one
```

12.2 Bit Operations

Bit operations include manipulations on the individual bits
within a register or memory location. One of the great
improvements of the Z-80 microprocessor over the 8080 is the
enormously increased number of bit operations that the Z-80
executes. There are many different kinds of bit operations.
They can be divided into the categories of rotate, shift, set,
reset, test, and BCD instructions.

12.3 Rotate and Shift Instructions

SHIFT instructions move the bits within a byte from one
position to the next, in a right or left direction. The bit
on the end of the byte in the direction of the shift is lost,
and a zero is shifted into the bit on the opposite end.
ROTATE instructions are identical to shift instructions,
except that the bit that would normally be lost is shifted
around to the other side. All rotate and shift instructions
on the Z-80 move only one bit, so that they need to be
repeated to move the bits more than one position.

    Shift and rotate instructions are complicated by the fact
that all of them use the carry bit in one way or another.
Sometimes the carry participates as an "extra" bit, producing
a 9-bit shift or rotate, and sometimes the carry is a
duplication of the end bit. ARITHMETIC shifts preserve the
SIGN bit (7) of the operand, whereas LOGICAL shifts have the
sign participate along with the other bits. (These are the
standard definitions of arithmetic and logical shifts. The
Z-80's SLA ("shift left arithmetic") instruction is really a
logical shift.) Most instructions are logical operations. We
will first review the instructions executed by the Z-80 and
then discuss applications.

    The first four instructions in this group are the only ones
also executed by the 8080. They only operate on the
accumulator, but they also require only one byte and execute

in 4 T cycles. They are therefore found in many existing programs:

mnemonic	description	operation
RLCA	rotate A left circular	8-bit rotate: bit 7 copied into both bit 0 and CY
RLA	rotate A left	9-bit rotate: bit 7 => CY, CY => bit 0
RRCA	rotate A right circular	8-bit rotate: bit 0 copied to both bit 7 and CY
RRA	rotate A right	9-bit rotate: bit 0 => CY, CY => bit 7

The remaining instructions, all Z-80 only, allow a myriad of operands. Any register (except F) may be specified, or any memory location addressed as (HL), (IX+d), or (IY+d). (There is some redundancy here in that A may be specified for these operations, duplicating the function of the instructions above.) We will list the rotate operations first, since they are identical to those above, except that they use different operands. In the following table, "s" means any register (A, B, C, D, E, H, or L) or (HL), (IX+d), or (IY+d):

mnemonic	description	operation
RLC s	rotate left circular	same as RLCA
RL s	rotate left	same as RLA
RRC s	rotate right circular	same as RRCA
RR s	rotate right	same as RRA

There are only three shift instructions on the Z-80, and they also allow any of the operands used for the above rotate instructions to be specified. One of the shifts is designated as a logical shift, and two shifts as arithmetic, even though the "arithmetic" left shift is really a logical shift as noted above. All of the shifts use the carry bit as a participant in the operation, in that the bit shifted off the end is shifted into the carry bit. These instructions are as follows:

mnemonic	description	operation
SLA s	shift left arithmetic	bits 0-7 shifted to bits 1-CY; bit 0=0
SRA s	shift right arithmetic	bits 7-0 shifted to bits 6-CY; bit 7 unchanged
SRL s	shift right logical	bits 7-0 shifted to bits 6-CY; bit 7=0

Shift and rotate instructions have many useful applications. One of their most obvious uses is in positioning the bits within a byte in order to perform some function. For example, to print the value of a byte in hexadecimal form, it is necessary first to print the left 4-bit digit, and then the right 4-bit digit. Converting a digit to ASCII form requires putting the value into the right four bits and adding an offset. If the value is between 0 and 9, the offset is 30H, but if it is between 10 and 15, the offset is 37H, because 37H + 10 = 41H (ASCII "A"). To move the left four bits over to the right, we could use the SRL operation four times in succession. This would automatically clear the right four bits, since zero is shifted into the left end. It would not necessarily be the best way of programming this function, however. Four SRL operations require 8 bytes and 32 T cycles to execute, assuming that the operand is in the accumulator. We could instead use four rotate instructions, and then mask out the left four bits with an AND instruction. Four RRA or RRCA operations require only 4 bytes and 16 T cycles, and the ensuing AND 0FH requires 2 bytes and 7 T cycles.

One of the most important applications of shift instructions is that of multiplication and division by powers of 2. When a byte is shifted left one bit, the value it contains is multiplied by 2, and when it is shifted right the value is divided by 2. This is illustrated by the following series of SLA operations:

decimal	CY	binary	hexadecimal	
5	-	0000 0101	0 5	original value
x 2=10	0	0000 1010	0 A	after 1st SLA
x 2=20	0	0001 0100	1 4	after 2nd SLA
x 2=40	0	0010 1000	2 8	after 3rd SLA
x 2=80	0	0101 0000	5 0	after 4th SLA
x 2=160	0	1010 0000	A 0	after 5th SLA
x 2=320	1	0100 0000	4 0	after 6th SLA

We can see that the result is no longer valid after the sixth SLA operation, because it should be a larger value than can be contained in a single byte. The carry bit can be used to test whether this condition has occurred, however, so that a subroutine that uses this method can take account of it. If we were using signed integers, the result would be incorrect after the fifth SLA, since a 1 was shifted into the sign bit. In this case, we would have to check the S flag (P or M conditions).

A more complicated extension of this principle can be used to implement a subroutine for multiplication by 10. This method depends on the fact that 10=8+2, both of which are powers of 2. The following sequence of instructions

multiplies the value in the accumulator by 10, using B to save
the value after the first shift:

```
        SLA     A           ;multiply by 2
        LD      B,A         ;save in B
        SLA     A           ;x 4
        SLA     A           ;x 8
        ADD     A,B         ;value x 8 + value x 2
```

Additional information about multiplication and division is
contained in chapter 13.

12.4 Bit Set, Reset, and Test Operations

SETTING a bit means setting it to 1.   RESETTING it means
setting   it   to   0.   TESTING a bit, which is done by the "BIT"
instructions,   means   a   test   for   zero,   the   result   being
indicated by the Z flag.   The important thing about these
instructions is that they allow the same large number of
operands   as   the   rotate   and   shift   instructions.   In the
following table, "s" indicates any of the operands A, B, C, D,
E, H, L, (HL), (IX+d), or (IY+d). "n" indicates the bit
number, which is 0 to 7:

mnemonic	description	operation
BIT n,s	bit test	test bit n in s
SET n,s	set bit	bit n in s set to 1
RES n,s	reset bit	bit n in s set to 0

These bit operations have many obvious applications.   One
of them is simply to use one byte as a test word for up to
eight "yes-no" options. 0 can indicate "no" and 1 "yes" (or
vice versa).   In our example of multiplication by 2 above, we
could test for the presence of the sign bit by a "BIT 7,A"
instruction.

12.5 BCD Operations

There are two special BCD rotate instructions that have highly
specialized applications.   (BCD numbers were described in
chapter 11.   They   consist   of   two 4-bit digits containing
values from 0 to 9 in each digit. For the purpose of these
operations,   the   digits can contain any values.) The two BCD
rotates, RLD and RRD, operate jointly on the contents of the
accumulator and on the memory location addressed by the HL
register pair, and they shift four bits at a time.   In each
case,   the   left four bits of A (bits 4-7) are unchanged, and
the remaining three digits,   contained   in bits 0-3 of A,
together with the two BCD digits in (HL), are shifted.   RRD

shifts to the right and RLD to the left.   The operation of these instructions can be diagrammed as follows (showing the contents as decimal digits rather than in binary form):

	A bits 4-7	0-3	(HL) bits 4-7	0-3
Original values	0	5	4	3
after RLD	0	4	3	5
original values (repeated)	0	5	4	3
after RRD	0	3	5	4

The uses of these operations are clearly restricted to specialized applications involving BCD numbers, which are not used by any of the standard TRS-80 software.

13

SOFTWARE MULTIPLICATION AND DIVISION

One of the greatest limitations of all 8-bit microprocessors is that they have no instructions that execute multiplication and division. Therefore, all such operations must be performed through programming, by means of repetitively executing additions and subtractions. This chapter is intended to show the reader how these operations are carried out in general, without covering the subject exhaustively. We will restrict our consideration to integer operations of various byte lengths. Multiplication and division are two of the most complicated and specialized subjects of microcomputer programming. Arithmetic computing ability is one of the few areas where the newer 16-bit microprocessors have a distinct advantage over the Z-80 and the 8080.

You may never have been aware of these limitations of the TRS-80, because Level II Basic executes all arithmetic operations -- even exponentiation. When you realize that Level II contains these facilities for three different number formats, you can better appreciate the extent to which its designers have gone for your convenience. The one thing you probably do notice, particularly about exponentiation, is that it takes a noticeable amount of time to execute. A few seconds to evaluate one complicated mathematical formula may correspond to millions of machine operations.

13.1   8-Bit Multiplication

First, let us note a few general points about multiplication.
The two numbers that are multiplied together are called the
MULTIPLIER and the MULTIPLICAND, and the result is called the
PRODUCT.   The   product   of two numbers of a given length may
require twice as many digits to contain the result (99 x 99 =
9801).   In binary terms, the product of two 8-bit numbers may
require 16 bits, and the product of two 16-bit numbers may
require 32 bits. (The maximum value that can be contained in
a byte is 255. 255 x 255 = 65025, which requires 16 bits but
is less than the maximum value that can be contained in 16
bits.) Any routines that we write for multiplication will
have to take this fact into account.

     When we learned to do arithmetic in school, we learned that
multiplication can be performed by repetitively adding one
number another number of times.   The most direct type of
multiplication subroutine can work in the same way. The
following example makes use of this method.   When it is
entered, the multiplicand is in A and the multiplier in B. The
result is returned in HL, to reflect the fact that the product
of two 8-bit numbers may extend to 16 bits, as mentioned
above.

```
;unsigned 8-bit multiplication subroutine
;on entry, A=multiplicand, B=multiplier
;on exit, HL=product, B=0
MULT8P  LD     L,A       ;multiplicand to L
        LD     H,0       ;zero high order bits
        INC    B         ;test B
        DEC    B         ;for zero
        JR     Z,ZERO    ;B=0
        DEC    B         ;if B=1,
        RET    Z         ;A=product
        PUSH   DE        ;save DE
        LD     D,H       ;move HL
        LD     E,L       ;to DE
MULOOP  ADD    HL,DE     ;add multiplicand
        DJNZ   MULOOP    ;continue B (-1) times
        POP    DE        ;restore DE
        RET              ;done
ZERO    LD     L,0       ;result is zero
        RET
```

     This subroutine works by placing the multiplicand into both
L and E, and clearing H and D. DE is added to HL (B-1) times.
If B=1, we return after loading HL because A times 1 is A.   If
B=0, the result is zero because anything times zero is zero.
The method of INCrementing and DECrementing B is a quick way

to test whether B is zero, without changing the values in any register.

One of the problems with this subroutine is that it is valid only for UNSIGNED numbers. If we want to take the sign bit into account, another procedure is necessary.   The simplest way of implementing signed multiplication is to check the signs on entry, do the multiplication on positive numbers as above, and readjust the sign on exit, if necessary.

The   following   subroutine   uses repetitive addition to perform 8-bit signed multiplication, using the same registers as above. The XOR operation is used to create the sign of the product ((+ x +) and (- x -) are both positive. Only (+ x -) and (- x +) are negative). OR A (which clears the carry bit and sets the condition codes to reflect the value of A without changing it) is used to test for positive or negative values.

```
;signed 8-bit multiplication by repetitive addition
;on entry, A=multiplicand, B=multiplier
;on exit, HL=product, B=0, A destroyed
MULT8   LD      L,A             ;save A temporarily
        LD      H,0             ;zero high bits
        INC     B               ;test for
        DEC     B               ;B=0
        RET     Z               ;product=0
        XOR     B               ;form product sign
        PUSH    AF              ;save sign in stack
        LD      A,B             ;test value of B
        OR      A
        JP      P,TSTA          ;if + skip
        NEG                     ;create positive equivalent
        LD      B,A             ;replace
TSTA    LD      A,L             ;retrieve A
        OR      A               ;test value
        JP      P,MUL           ;if +
        NEG                     ;positive equivalent
        LD      L,A             ;replace in L
MUL     DEC     B               ;if B=1,
        JR      Z,ADJUST        ;product=multiplicand
        PUSH    DE              ;save DE
        LD      D,H             ;move HL
        LD      E,L             ;to DE
        ADD     HL,DE           ;add multiplicand
        DJNZ    $-1             ;continue till B=0
        POP     DE              ;restore DE
ADJUST  POP     AF              ;retrieve sign
        OR      A               ;test sign of product
        RET     P               ;ok if plus
        LD      A,L             ;form negative equivalent
        CPL                     ;complement
        LD      L,A             ;replace in L
```

```
        LD      A,H                 ;do same with H
        CPL
        LD      H,A                 ;replace
        INC     HL                  ;NEG=CPL+1
        RET                         ;done
```

     While multiplication by repetitive addition does work, it
is extremely slow compared with other ways of implementing the
operation.   It should be used only when small numbers are
being multiplied. The usual way in which multiplication is
carried out involves a process similar to the paper-and-pencil
method of performing the operation, where you align the
product of each additional digit one position to the left to
indicate that it is a greater power of 10, such as in the
following examples:

```
                123                         456
              x 456                       x 123
              -----                       -----
                738                        1368
                615                         912
                492                         456
              ------                      ------
              56088                       56088
```

A binary multiplication might be written out as follows:

```
           binary          hexadecimal        decimal
        0010 1011              2BH               43
      x 0001 0101              15H               21
        ---------              ----              ---
        0010 1011              387H              43
      0 0000 000                                 86
     00 1010 11                                  ---
    000 0000 0                                   903
   0010 1011
   --------------
   0011 1000 0111
```

     Note that it is very easy to write out the product of a
binary number, because the result is either the original
number or zero. In the first, third, and fifth rows above, we
have the same number, the multiplicand, the only difference
being the vertical alignment. Spaces are placed every four
bits to increase readibility.

     This method of multiplication, shown below, makes use of
the fact that when you add the value in the HL register pair
to itself, the result is shifted left one bit:

H	L	hexadecimal	decimal
0000 1010	0010 1011	0A2BH	2603
0000 1010	0010 1011	0A2BH	2603
----------	-----------	-----	----
0001 0100	0101 0110	1456H	5206

The subroutine below uses this principle to create unsigned multiplication, as above. The bits of the multiplier are tested successively, and the multiplicand is added to the product if the tested bit is one. If it is zero, the addition is skipped. The product is then shifted left to be in position for the next bit. This subroutine uses the same registers as those above.

```
;unsigned 8-bit multiplication
;on entry, A=multiplier, B=multiplicand
;on exit, HL=product, B=0, A destroyed
MULT8P  PUSH    DE              ;save DE
        LD      E,B             ;multiplicand to E (LSB)
        LD      D,0             ;clear high bits of DE
        LD      B,8             ;8 bit multiply
        LD      HL,0            ;zap product
MULOOP  ADD     HL,HL           ;shift product left 1 bit
        RLCA                    ;shift multiplier bit into C
        JR      NC,MULP2        ;skip addition if zero
        ADD     HL,DE           ;else add multiplicand
MULP2   DJNZ    MULOOP          ;continue through 8 bits
        POP     DE              ;restore DE
        RET                     ;done
```

13.2 16-Bit Multiplication

16-bit multiplication can be carried out in a manner exactly analogous to 8-bit multiplication, as long as we remember that the product may have to occupy 32 bits. If we want to implement a practical method for 16-bit operations, as in Level II Basic integer arithmetic, then we would say that OVERFLOW exists when the product requires more than 16 bits. This could either cause an error condition, or we could simply use the 16 low-order bits, producing a result modulo 65536.

The following subroutine performs unsigned 16-bit multiplication, on a multiplier and multiplicand contained in the BC and DE register pairs. The low-order bits of the product are returned in HL, and the high-order or overflow bits in DE. It is the calling program's responsibility to test DE for zero to determine whether overflow has occurred, and proceed appropriately. This subroutine uses A as a counter for the number of bits in the operation, and uses the

more efficient method of shifting the product left for each
successive bit rather than repetitive addition.

```
;16-bit unsigned multiplication
;on entry, BC=multiplicand, DE=multiplier
;on exit, product in DE (high-order) and HL (low-order)
MULT16  LD      A,16            ;bit count
        LD      HL,0            ;zero initial product
MLT1    ADD     HL,HL           ;shift product left 1 bit
        RL      E               ;shift low product to carry
        RL      D               ;multiplier bit to carry
        JR      NC,MLT2         ;skip if multiplier bit 0
        ADD     HL,BC           ;else add multiplicand
        JR      NC,MLT2         ;skip if no carry to hi bits
        INC     E               ;increment 3rd byte
        JR      NZ,MLT2         ;skip if no carry to 4th byte
        INC     D               ;increment 4th byte
MLT2    DEC     A               ;bit count
        JR      NZ,MLT1         ;continue till 0
        RET                     ;done
```

The "RL E" operation shifts the left bit of register E into
the carry, and the immediately following "RL D" shifts the bit
from the carry into bit 0 of D and bit 7 of D to the carry.
This is, in effect, a double-precision left shift. The last
bit shifted into D is the bit that we test for the
multiplication, and if it is zero we skip the intervening
steps. Once the multiplicand has been added, we have to find
out if there is a carry to the third or fourth bytes. Since
the "ADD HL,BC" operation produces a carry in this case, all
we need to do is to test the carry bit after this operation.
If there is one, E is incremented, and then we need to know if
there is a carry from E to D. Unfortunately, the "INC E"
operation does not affect the carry, but the only time a carry
would be needed would be when the value of E was 1111 1111
binary, producing zero after the incrementing. We can
therefore test the zero flag in this instance.

Signed 16-bit multiplication can be done in the same manner
as signed 8-bit multiplication, the only additional
complication being that negation of the product must be
carried out on all four bytes of the result. The following
subroutine carries out this procedure, using the same
registers as above.

```
;signed 16-bit multiplication
;on entry, multiplier and multiplicand in BC and DE
;on exit, product in DE + HL
MPY16   LD      A,B             ;determine product sign
        XOR     D               ;sign in bit 7 of high byte
        PUSH    AF              ;save sign in stack
```

```
          LD       A,B              ;test sign
          OR       A                ;of multiplier
          JP       P,MPY1           ;skip if positive
          LD       HL,Ø             ;negate BC by subtracting
                                    ;from zero.  No need to clear
          SBC      HL,BC            ;carry because of prev. OR A
          LD       B,H              ;transfer HL
          LD       C,L              ;to BC
MPY1      LD       A,D              ;test sign
          OR       A                ;of multiplicand
          JP       P,MPY2           ;ok if plus
          LD       HL,Ø             ;negate DE
          SBC      HL,DE            ;by subtracting from zero
          EX       DE,HL            ;transfer to DE by exchange
MPY2      LD       A,16             ;bit count
          LD       HL,Ø             ;initial product
MPY3      ADD      HL,HL            ;same method as above
          RL       E                ; (see comments above)
          RL       D
          JR       NC,MPY4
          ADD      HL,BC
          JR       NC,MPY4
          INC      E
          JR       NZ,MPY4
          INC      D
MPY4      DEC      A
          JR       NZ,MPY3
          POP      AF               ;retrieve sign of product
          OR       A                ;test it
          RET      P                ;done if plus
          XOR      A                ;form negative equivalent
          SUB      L                ;by subtraction from zero
          LD       L,A              ;replace L
          LD       A,Ø              ;clears A but not carry
          SBC      A,H              ;propagate carry to 2nd byte
          LD       H,A              ;replace H
          LD       A,Ø              ;clear A but not carry
          SBC      A,E              ;3rd byte
          LD       E,A              ;replace
          LD       A,Ø              ;clear A but not carry
          ABC      A,D              ;4th byte
          LD       D,A              ;replace
          RET                       ;done
```

This subroutine uses the method of producing a negative equivalent of a positive number by subtracting it from zero. The negation of the product propagates the carry bit through four bytes (from L to H to E to D).

13.3   8-Bit Division

When division is performed, a number called the DIVIDEND is divided by the DIVISOR, producing a QUOTIENT and a REMAINDER. As long as we are restricting our consideration to integers, we have only to return these two values and not worry about their meaning. When performing division, we have the opposite situation from multiplication with regard to the magnitude of the numbers involved. A 16-bit dividend may be divided by an 8-bit divisor to produce an 8-bit quotient. There is one consideration that must be taken into account here. The quotient must be able to be contained in 8 bits. If this is not true, a DIVIDE FAULT condition exists. In addition, the divisor must not be zero -- at least, in any subroutine that we write for division, we must guard against causing the program to go into an infinite loop on a divide-by-zero.

As with multiplication, the simplest kind of division to understand is a method that uses successive subtractions. The following subroutine parallels the unsigned 8-bit multiplication above. On entry, HL contains the dividend and A the divisor. On exit, the quotient is returned in B and the remainder in L. The previous value of DE is lost.

```
;unsigned 8-bit division
;on entry, HL=dividend, A=divisor
;on exit, B=quotient, L=remainder, DE destroyed
DIV8P   OR      A               ;test A for zero
        JR      Z,DZERO         ;divide by zero
        LD      B,Ø             ;zero initial quotient
        LD      E,A             ;divisor to low bits of DE
        LD      D,Ø             ;zero high bits
DIVLP   OR      A               ;clear carry
        SBC     HL,DE           ;subtract divisor
        JP      M,REM           ;if negative, done
        INC     B               ;increment quotient
        JR      DIVLP           ;continue
REM     ADD     HL,DE           ;find remainder
        RET                     ;done
DZERO   ...                     ;set error code
```

This subroutine makes no effort to catch a divide fault condition. It simply allows the process to continue by incrementing B until HL goes negative. Therefore, the result is actually the quotient modulo 256, and may be incorrect.

The method of successive subtraction is also very slow, and a process of shifting, similar to that for multiplication, can be implemented instead. The following subroutine achieves the same result as that above, but uses only eight subtractions. The quotient is returned in L and the remainder in H.

```
;unsigned 8-bit division
;on entry, HL=dividend, A=divisor
;on exit, L=quotient, H=remainder
DIV8P   LD      B,8             ;bit count
        LD      E,0             ;clear low-order byte
        LD      D,A             ;DE=divisor
DV1     ADD     HL,HL           ;shift divisor left
        SBC     HL,DE           ;subtract divisor
        JR      C,DV2           ;if C then high dvdnd < dvsr
        INC     HL              ;if NC set quotient bit to 1
        JR      DV3             ;skip following add
DV2     ADD     HL,DE           ;restore high dividend
DV3     DJNZ    DV1             ;continue for 8 bits
        RET                     ;done
```

The "ADD HL,HL" at DV1 clears the lowest bit of L, which
will be used to hold the quotient bit. Note that the
subtraction of the divisor affects only the high-order byte,
because we placed it into D and cleared E before starting. If
the subtract produces a carry, then the high-order dividend
was less than the divisor -- in other words, the subtract was
not valid. In this instance, the bits are restored by the
following "ADD HL,DE".

Now let us examine the divide fault condition more
carefully. First, the highest bit of the dividend must not be
a one, at least if the above method is used, because the "ADD
HL,HL" will shift it out into the carry, before the first
subtraction. Second, the divisor cannot be zero. In the
remaining instances, the divide fault can exist only if the
high-order byte of HL (H) is equal to or greater than the
divisor (A). Some examples will clarify this:

```
             HL = 16384              4000H
              A =    48                30H
  16384 / 48 =   341  R 16           155H


             HL = 28672              7000H
              A =    64                40H
  18672 / 64 =   448  R 0            1C0H


             HL = 28672              7000H
              A =   112                70H
 28672 / 112 =   256  R 0            100H


             HL = 16384              4000H
              A =    80                50H
  28672 / 80 =   204  R 64           CCH
```

Each of the quotients in the first three examples are
greater than 255, requiring an additional byte. This byte

comparison of A with H can be used as a method of checking for a divide fault. The following is an extension of the preceding subroutine: when added to the beginning, it will jump to the location DFAULT (not shown) if the divide fault condition exists, otherwise proceed as before.

```
;check for divide fault condition
DIV8F   BIT     7,H             ;test high bit of H
        JR      NZ,DFAULT       ;divide fault if 1
        CP      H               ;compare high dvdnd, divisor
        JR      C,DIV8P         ;ok if divisor less
        JR      DFAULT          ;else divide fault
DIV8P   ...                     ;(as above)
```

The "JR C,DIV8P" also takes care of the situation where A is zero, because in that case H cannot be less than A.

13.4 16-Bit Division

By 16-bit division, we mean of course division of a 32-bit dividend by a 16-bit divisor producing a quotient and remainder of 16 bits each. A subroutine to perform this operation is a simple extension of the 8-bit subroutines above. The following subroutine divides the 32-bit dividend in H, L, B, and C by the 16-bit divisor in DE. The quotient is returned in BC and the remainder in HL. If there is a divide fault, the program jumps to location DFAULT (not shown).

```
;16-bit unsigned division
;on entry, dividend in H,L,B,C (highest to lowest),
;divisor in DE
;on exit, quotient in BC, remainder in HL, A=0
DIV16   BIT     7,H             ;test highest divident bit
        JR      NZ,DFAULT       ;divide fault if 1
        PUSH    HL              ;save high dividend bytes
        PUSH    DE              ;save divisor
        OR      A               ;clear carry
        SBC     HL,DE           ;subt. divisor frm hi dvdnd
        JR      NC,DFAULT       ;fault if NC
        POP     DE              ;get back divisor
        POP     HL              ;get back high dividend
        LD      A,16            ;bit count
DIVD1   SLA     C               ;shift dividend left
        RL      B               ;shift into B
        ADC     HL,HL           ;add HL + carry from B
        SBC     HL,DE           ;subtract divisor
        JR      NC,DIVD2        ;ok if no carry
        ADD     HL,DE           ;else add back
        JR      DIVD3           ;try next bit
```

```
DIVD2    INC    C                    ;set quotient bit to 1
DIVD3    DEC    A                    ;decrement bit count
         JR     NZ,DIVD1             ;continue 16 times
         RET                         ;done;
```

The "SLA C" shifts the lowest byte of the dividend left, clearing bit 0 and shifting bit 7 into the carry. The following "RL B" shifts the carry into bit 0 of B, thus making this a 16-bit shift. The following "ADC HL,HL" shifts HL left one bit, but it also picks up the carry from bit 7 of B. The bit vacated by the "SLA C" is where the quotient is stored, and the quotient is propagated into B by the double left shift.

A 16-bit signed divide subroutine is not shown, although it is a simple matter to construct one using the same method shown above for 8-bit division.

14
CASSETTE INPUT AND OUTPUT

Transferring data between memory and the cassette tape recorder is similar to reading the keyboard or displaying characters on the video monitor. It is not really necessary for a programmer to know how such a transfer works, as long as he knows how to use the ROM subroutines that carry out the essential operations. One important difference between the keyboard and video display on the one hand, and the cassette recorder on the other, is that the former are memory mapped, whereas the cassette recorder is interfaced through an input/output port, number 255 (hexadecimal FF), which also controls the 32- or 64-character mode of the video display. Thus, only certain bits of this port are used. The disks and line printer are also memory-mapped, whereas the RS-232-C interface and various other peripherals are interfaced through ports. The TRS-80 has much room for expansion of input and output devices using either method.

The addresses of ROM subroutines that are used for cassette input and output have been mentioned above in chapter 5, but they will be reviewed here in more detail. All are located between addresses 01D9H and 0313H. ("H" is often appended to addresses to remind you that they are hexadecimal numbers.)

14.1   Cassette ROM Subroutines

Address	Function
01F8H	Turns cassette off. Uses register A.
0212H	"Define drive": A=0 for cassette 1 or 1 for cassette 2. Turns on the proper cassette drive and selects it for subsequent operations.
0235H	Read byte, which is returned in A. Uses no other registers.
0264H	Write byte in A to cassette. Uses no other registers.
0287H	Write leader and sync byte. Uses AF, C.
0296H	Read leader and sync byte. Uses AF. Two asterisks appear in the upper right corner of the video display when leader and sync byte are found.
0314H	Reads two bytes (LSB/MSB) and transfers to HL. Uses AF.

All cassette input and output operations in assembly language can be done using these subroutines.   All standard tape formats are readable. Some programmers have developed non-standard methods that encode the bits in some different way.   These operations are beyond the scope of this discussion.

The beginning of a file on the cassette tape is signified by a "leader and sync byte", which is actually a succession of 255 zeros followed by A5 (the sync byte). Each bit of data is read from the tape separately. This means that the timing of the routine that reads the bits is extremely crucial. This is why you must disable interrupts (CMD"T") in Disk Basic when reading cassettes. It is also why TRS-80 owners who have had the clock speed modified must switch to the older, slower speed in order to read standard cassette tapes.

Once the cassette tape is turned on and the leader and sync byte located or written, it is the programmer's responsibility to keep up with the speed of the cassette in order to read or write data properly. (Writing data may be less crucial than reading it.) The data-transfer speed of the cassette is 500 baud ("baud" means "bits per second"), so that a bit must be read or written every 2 milliseconds.   What this means is that, for most purposes, all you can do is to read or write data into or out of memory and stop the cassette when you want to do some computation. Each time you stop the cassette, you must start it again with a leader and sync byte combination, to make sure that no data is lost due to the start and stop motion of the cassette. Any program that does not keep up with the 500-baud data transfer rate will lose bits of data, thus reading incorrect values.

14.2 Tape Formats

To keep up with the cassette's speed, standard tape formats have been developed by Radio Shack to indicate what the data on the tape represents, where it goes, when to stop the cassette, and what to do after stopping. There are four standard tape formats: Basic programs, Basic data, machine-language object tapes (the SYSTEM format), and Editor/Assembler symbolic-program files. Other formats, such as data files for the Electric Pencil program, have been devised for various reasons, but will not be discussed here.

1. Machine Language Object (SYSTEM) Tapes

An "object program" is a program in machine code ready to run on a computer. When stored on an external medium such as a cassette tape, it is necessary only to dump it into memory and jump to the starting location.

The object-program format is also known as the SYSTEM format because of the Basic command used to read such tapes. Data is written on the tape in the form of blocks less than 256 bytes in length. Each block begins with a header byte identifying what kind of block it is. There are three types of blocks: FILENAME, DATA, and ENTRY. FILENAME is first, followed by any number of DATA blocks. The ENTRY block comes last, after which the cassette is turned off. The whole tape has the following structure:

```
(Leader and Sync Byte)
Filename Header        55H
File Name              6 bytes (ASCII), filled with
                       blanks if name less than 6
                       characters.
Data Header            3CH
Count Byte             Number of data bytes to
                       follow (1-256)
Load Address           2 bytes, LSB/MSB, indicating
                       where data is to be loaded
(Other Data Blocks)
Entry Header           78H
Entry Address          2 bytes, LSB/MSB.
```

The fact that each data block has its own address means that data can be loaded anywhere in memory, and that the same tape can contain data that goes into several different areas. Usually, only the Editor/Assembler program produces such tapes (through the use of different ORG statements), because monitors such as TBUG or Monitors 3 and 4 (as well as the TAPEDISK utility program) require that you specify one

contiguous block. If the checksum is wrong, or if the header
byte is not 55, 3C, or 78, an error is produced.   If reading
the cassette under SYSTEM, a "C" replaces one of the asterisks
in the upper right corner.

2.   Editor/Assembler Source Program Tapes

    Source tapes for the Editor/Assembler program have a format
different from other tapes:

          (Leader and Sync Byte)
          Filename Header   D3H
          File Name   6 bytes (ASCII), padded with
                                blanks

          Individual program statements:
          Line Number   5 bytes, ASCII-encoded,
                                with bit 7 (parity) set
          Statement Code   (Any length). TAB (right
                                arrow) key encoded as Ø9.
          Carriage Return   ØD (ENTER key)
          (Last statement - END - encoded in same manner)

          End Byte   1AH (shift down-arrow)

    This format is essentially a dump of the memory   area   that
holds   the   source   program   when running the Editor/Assembler
program, except that when the program resides in memory, the
line numbers are stored in two bytes (LSB/MSB). The tape thus
takes more room than the program in memory. This is also the
format used to hold symbolic files on disk.

3.   Level II Basic Program Tapes

    A   Level II Basic program tape is essentially a dump of the
program as it is stored in memory. This is not the way in
which you type it in, nor the way it is listed when you print
it, because all of the key words are translated into a binary
code.   Statement numbers are stored in two bytes. This is why
they may have a maximum value of 65529 (65535 less a few
values used for special purposes). The only recognizable data
is the ASCII text in PRINT statements, variable names, and
constants. The complete format is as follows:

```
(Leader and Sync Byte)
Header                        D3 D3 D3
File Name                     First byte only, ASCII
Program Statements            Starts loading directly into
                              42E9H (Level II)
                              or 68BAH (Disk Basic)
End Flag                      00 00 00
```

This is also the standard format used to store Basic programs on disk, except that disk storage also provides the "ASCII" option (SAVE "PGM",A), which stores the program in exactly the same way that it is printed by a LIST command.

4. Level II Basic Data Tapes

Because of the one important point mentioned above -- that you must write a new leader and sync byte each time that you start or stop the cassette -- Level II Basic data tapes are stored in a very inefficient manner. Each time a PRINT #-1 or INPUT #-1 is executed, a new leader and sync byte is written or read. A Basic program can take advantage of this situation, by trying to include as much data as possible within a single statement, but it is impossible to escape the fact that most of the time is spent reading the leader and sync bytes.

The exact format of a data tape is so simple that a table is not necessary. After the leader and sync byte comes the data itself, terminating in a carriage return. Individual items in the list are separated by commas. For this reason a comma cannot be included in a string saved on cassette tape (nor can a carriage return). Strings are written simply as a series of characters. All numbers, whether they represent integers or single- or double-precision values, are stored as ASCII strings surrounded by blank spaces. Thus, a number could be written as an integer and read as a single- or double-precision number or string. The decimal point is included if present. A string consisting of numerals can be written as a string and read as a number, but if it contains any non-numerical characters, an error is produced. The warning in the LEVEL II BASIC REFERENCE MANUAL is not totally correct. It is possible to read data in some form other than that in which it was written, but you must always read the same number of items. The carriage-return character (0DH) is the cue to stop the cassette when data is being read.

14.3 Programming Cassette Input and Output

The most useful format for an assembly-language programmer is that for machine-language object tapes. Using this format, both programs and data can be saved, as long as they are read into or out of a contiguous memory block. The program shown below reads an object tape into memory, even blinking the asterisk in the upper right corner like the SYSTEM command. Rather than having you specify the name, however, the name is read off the tape and printed on the video display. When the program has been read completely, the starting, ending, and entry addresses are also printed. The program then waits for you to type a key. If you type ENTER, execution of the program read into memory begins. Otherwise, the system is rebooted.

```
;PROGRAM TO READ MACHINE-LANGUAGE OBJECT TAPES
REBOOT  EQU     Ø               ;ROM ADDRESSES
VIDEO   EQU     33H
INPUT   EQU     49H
CASOFF  EQU     1F8H
DEFDRV  EQU     212H
RSYNC   EQU     296H
RBYTE   EQU     235H
RHL     EQU     314H
        ORG     7EØØH           ;NEAR TOP OF 16K
START   CALL    CLS             ;CLEAR SCREEN AT START
READY   LD      HL,FREADY       ;PRINT "READY CASSETTE"
        CALL    PRINT
        CALL    INPUT           ;WAIT FOR KEYIN
        LD      HL,FNAME        ;MESSAGE
        CALL    PRINT
        XOR     A               ;CASSETTE 1
        CALL    DEFDRV
        CALL    RSYNC
        CALL    RBYTE           ;FIRST BYTE
        CP      55H             ;FILENAME HEADER
        JR      NZ,CERR         ;WRONG TAPE IF NOT
        LD      B,6             ;6-LETTER NAME
        CALL    RBYTE
        CALL    DISP            ;PRINT ON SCREEN
        DJNZ    $-6
        CALL    RBYTE           ;FIRST BLOCK
        CALL    RDH
        LD      (ADR1),HL       ;SAVE 1ST LOC
        JR      CLP2
CLP     CALL    RBYTE           ;1ST BYTE OF BLOCK
        CP      78H             ;ENTRY?
        JR      Z,CEND
        CALL    RHD
```

```
CLP2     ADD     A,L              ;COMPUTE CHECKSUM
         LD      C,A              ;SAVE IN C
CRD      CALL    RBYTE            ;READ DATA
         LD      (HL),A           ;SAVE IN MEMORY
         ADD     A,C              ;COMPUTE CHECKSUM
         LD      C,A              ;SAVE IN C
         INC     HL               ;NEXT LOC
         DJNZ    CRD              ;CONTINUE THRU BLOCK
         CALL    RBYTE            ;CHECKSUM FROM TAPE
         CP      C                ;OK?
         JR      NZ,CHKSM         ;IF NOT, BAD READ
         PUSH    HL
         LD      HL,3C3FH         ;RIGHT CORNER OF VIDEO
         LD      A,'*'            ;BLINK
         CP      (HL)             ;IF '*' ALREADY THERE,
         JR      NZ,$+4           ;CHANGE TO
         LD      A,' '            ;BLANK
         LD      (HL),A           ;STORE
         POP     HL
         JR      CLP              ;GET NEXT BLOCK
CHKSM    LD      HL,FCHKSM        ;CHECKSUM ERROR
         JR      $+5
CERR     LD      HL,FCERR         ;READ ERROR
         CALL    PRINT
         CALL    CASOFF           ;STOP TAPE
         JR      READY            ;TRY AGAIN
CEND     LD      (ADR2),HL        ;ENDING ADDRESS
         CALL    RHL              ;GET ENTRY ADDRESS
         LD      (ADR3),HL        ;SAVE
         CALL    CASOFF           ;STOP
         LD      HL,(ADR1)        ;PRINT ADDRESSES
         CALL    PHL              ;START
         LD      HL,(ADR2)        ;END
         CALL    PHL
         LD      HL,(ADR3)        ;ENTRY
         CALL    PHL
         CALL    INPUT            ;WAIT FOR KEYIN
         CP      13               ;ENTER KEY
         JP      NZ,REBOOT        ;REBOOT IF NOT
         JP      (HL)             ;ELSE EXECUTE PROGRAM
RHD      CP      3CH              ;CODE FOR DATA BLOCK
         JR      NZ,CERR          ;IF NOT DATA, NOGOOD
         CALL    RBYTE            ;LENGTH
         LD      B,A              ;SAVE IN B
         JP      RHL              ;GET ADDRESS, RETURN
PRINT    LD      A,(HL)           ;PRINT MESSAGE
         AND     7FH              ;MASK PARITY
         CALL    DISP
         BIT     7,(HL)           ;DONE IF NZ
         RET     NZ
         INC     HL               ;NEXT LOC
```

```
        JR      PRINT           ;CONTINUE
PHL     LD      A,' '           ;PRINT
        CALL    DISP            ;TWO
        CALL    DISP            ;SPACES
        LD      A,H             ;PRINT H
        CALL    HEX             ;AND L
        LD      A,L             ;IN HEX
HEX     PUSH    AF
        RRCA
        RRCA
        RRCA
        RRCA
        CALL    HEX2
        POP     AF
HEX2    AND     15
        ADD     A,30H
        CP      3AH
        JR      C,DISP
        ADD     A,7
DISP    CALL    VIDEO
        RET
;FORMATS
FREADY  DEFM    'READY CASSETTE'
        DEFB    8DH
FCERR   DEFM    'CASSETTE READ ERROR'
        DEFB    8DH
FCHKSM  DEFM    'CHECKSUM ERROR'
        DEFB    8DH
FNAME   DEFM    'NAME    START END    ENTRY'
        DEFB    8DH
;DATA AREAS
ADR1    DEFS    2               ;START
ADR2    DEFS    2               ;END
ADR3    DEFS    2               ;ENTRY
        END     START
```

   This program contains four utility subroutines and one
specialized subroutine. The utility subroutines are DISP,
which displays a byte on the video screen (note that it is not
necessary to save DE and IY, because they are not used); HEX,
which prints the byte in A in hexadecimal form;   PHL, which
prints two spaces followed by the bytes in H and L in
hexadecimal form; and PRINT, which displays an ASCII message
until a byte with bit 7 set is found. At the end of the
program, there are four messages printed by this subroutine
(FREADY, FCERR, FCHKSM, and FNAME). Each message terminates
in the byte 8DH, which represents the carriage return with bit
7 set.

The program begins by printing "READY CASSETTE" and waiting for you to type a key. It then prints a message indicating the information it will give you about the tape it reads (name and starting, ending, and entry addresses). After getting the tape going, it checks to see whether the first byte is 55H, which is the code for file name. If not, the wrong type of tape is being read. The address of the first block must be saved for the message later. For this reason, the portion of the program that checks to see if a data block is occurring as expected, and reads the length and address of the block, is made into a subroutine (RHD). The block is read and checksum computed. At the conclusion of the block read, the checksum computed is compared to that on the tape. If they are not identical, an error has occurred. Any tape error results in the program being restarted from the "READY CASSETTE" message.

The asterisk blinks only at the end of a block. If an asterisk is already present in the upper right corner of the video display, it is changed to a blank. Otherwise an asterisk is stored there. After the entry block has been read, the tape is stopped and the addresses displayed. The program is then executed if you type ENTER.

Suppose that you have a tape written in some non-standard format that you want to know how to read. How can you discover what is on the tape? The following program can be used for this purpose. All it does is read the bytes off the tape directly into memory, starting at 7026H (BUFFER). It never stops, so you must press the RESET button when you think it is done. After hitting RESET, you can use a program such as Monitor 3 or 4 or SUPERZAP to examine the contents of memory and see what is on the tape. This method was in fact used to work out the tape formats described above.

```
;PROGRAM TO READ A CASSETTE TAPE DIRECTLY INTO MEMORY
DEFDRV  EQU     212H
RSYNC   EQU     296H
RBYTE   EQU     235H
BLINK   EQU     3C3FH                   ;UPPER RIGHT CORNER
        ORG     7000H
START   DI                              ;SAME AS CMD"T"
        XOR     A                       ;START TAPE
        CALL    DEFDRV
        CALL    RSYNC
        LD      DE,BLINK                ;SET UP BLINKING
        LD      B,'*'
        EXX
        LD      B,' '
        EXX
```

```
        LD      HL,BUFFER                ;WHERE TO PUT DATA
READ    CALL    RBYTE                    ;GET BYTE
        LD      (HL),A                   ;STORE
        INC     HL                       ;NEXT LOC
        LD      A,B                      ;GET BLINK CHAR
        LD      (DE),A                   ;BLINK
        CALL    RBYTE                    ;NEXT BYTE
        LD      (HL),A                   ;STORE
        INC     HL                       ;NEXT LOC
        EXX                              ;GET OTHER BLINK CHAR
        LD      A,B
        EXX
        LD      (DE),A                   ;BLINK
        JR      READ                     ;CONTINUE
BUFFER  DEFS    1                        ;TO END OF MEMORY
        END     START
```

You may wonder why it was not possible simply to read the tape directly to the video display itself, rather than having to save it in memory. The reason is that the computation involved in converting the data to hexadecimal form is too lengthy for the computer to keep up with the 500-baud tape speed. The computation involved in blinking the asterisk in this example, which consists of loading an asterisk into B and a blank into B', and then alternately storing B or B' in the upper right corner, is an example of the kind of computation that can be carried out when reading data from cassettes.

Recently, some companies have been selling programs that come with a special tape-loading program that uses a non-standard format, to prevent you from listing or saving the program. This prevents people from making pirated copies of the software. The program above, coupled with a disassembler, can be used to discover the method actually used to load the programs, and ultimately to read them yourself. While reading such tapes is certainly possible, understanding how these loaders work is a much more complicated task, beyond the scope of this discussion.

This information is a testimony that there is no mystery of the TRS-80 is beyond the power of a person who understands assembly-language programming. Nevertheless, we do not encourage people to discover how to make pirate copies of software, which is a serious problem in the microcomputer industry today.

15

USR SUBROUTINES IN BASIC PROGRAMS

15.1 USR Subroutines

One of the most practical applications of assembly-language
programming is to carry out some of the operations of a Basic
program.   The USR statement is the means by which assembly-
language subroutines can be called from Basic.   The USR
subroutine must be located at the top of your RAM in order for
it to be protected, and you must set the memory size to the
first location used by the subroutine.   Calling a USR
subroutine requires a different procedure in Level II and Disk
Basic.

The procedure for calling a USR subroutine in Level II
Basic is so confusing that there was an error in the first
edition of the REFERENCE MANUAL in the illustration.   It is
actually very simple.   All you have to do is to put the
address of the location you want to call into locations 408EH
and 408FH as a two-byte integer. The complicated aspect of
this is that the numbers must be POKEd into these locations,
one byte at a time, in decimal form. The decimal equivalent
of 408EH is 16526 and that of 408FH is 16527.   To know what to
POKE into these locations, you need to convert each byte of
the entry address of the subroutine into decimal form, and
then put the least-significant byte into 16526 and the most-
significant byte into 16527. Suppose that the entry address
is 7D00H.   The first byte is 7D and the second 00.   7DH is 125
and 00 is 0.   You must therefore POKE 0 into 16526 and 125

into 16527. Then the execution of a "X=USR(N)" statement will
cause a CALL to location 7D00H to be executed.

This procedure is much simpler in Disk Basic, because there
are ten USR functions and the entry location is set by the
DEFUSR statement.   In addition, hexadecimal constants are
allowed. Instead of all that conversion from hexadecimal to
decimal and POKEing into 16526 and 16527, all you have to do
is to say DEFUSR0=&H7D00. If you are using Disk Basic, you
probably have 32 or 48K RAM available, and you will therefore
probably locate the subroutines up in high memory, such as
&HFD00. for 48K.

One integer (2-byte) argument, specified in the parentheses
following the USR or USRn, may be passed to the USR subroutine
in the calling statement. Additional arguments may be POKEd
into RAM locations inside the USR subroutine, or anywhere
within the protected memory area.

If you want the USR subroutine to operate upon variables
used by the Basic program, you need to tell it where those
variables are located.   This is the purpose of the VARPTR
statement. VARPTR(X) returns the address of the first byte of
the variable X.   Integer variables require 2 bytes, single-
precision variables 4, double-precision 8, and strings 3 plus
the length of the string (0 to 255 bytes). PEEK(VARPTR(X))
gets the actual value itself, but an assembly-language
subroutine will usually want the address rather than the
data.

The only problem with passing a VARPTR argument to a USR
subroutine comes when you need to pass more than one of them,
so that you must use the "POKE" method mentioned above. In
this situation, you have to break down the VARPTR address into
two bytes and POKE them into the respective locations. Here,
you can use an extra integer variable to simplify the process.
In the following example, suppose that you want to pass the
address of the variable X to a USR subroutine by POKEing it
into locations 7FFEH and 7FFFH (32766 and 32767). You can use
an extra variable Y for this purpose:

```
        110 DEFINT Y
        120 Y=VARPTR(X)
        130 POKE 32766,PEEK(VARPTR(Y))
        140 POKE 32767,PEEK(VARPTR(Y)+1)
```

PEEK(VARPTR(Y)) contains the first (least-significant) byte of
the address of X, and PEEK(VARPTR(Y)+1) the second (most-
significant) byte. Y must be defined as an integer, but X may
be any type of variable. Y can now be re-used in the program,
since it is only needed temporarily.

If the variable whose address you want to pass to the assembly-language program is subscripted, you need only pass the address of the first location used (usually subscript 0 or 1).   You can then rely on the fact that if A(0) is stored in one series of bytes, A(1) will be in the next, A(2) will follow A(1), etc. The amount that you have to increment the address depends on the type of variable.   For integers, single-, and double-precision numbers, this amount is 2, 4, and 8 bytes, respectively. The data itself is stored in these contiguous locations.   For strings, the amount is 3 bytes. The information stored there is the length of the string in the first byte and its address in the following two bytes. The data itself is stored elsewhere, in the string space area (reserved by the CLEAR statement).

A single argument may also be passed back to the Basic program.   This is stored in the variable on the left side of the equals sign that has USR on the right.   X=USR(0) passes the argument 0 to the subroutine, and when it returns, the value passed from the subroutine back to the Basic program is stored in X.   The HL register pair is used to hold the argument in both cases.

If you want to pick up the argument when entering the assembly-language subroutine, you must first CALL 0A7FH.   To pass the argument back to the Basic program, you must terminate the program with a jump (JP) to location 0A9AH (2714).   If you don't want to return an argument, you simply RET (return) at the end of your subroutine.

15.2 Sorting a Series of Integers

Sorting an array of numbers is one operation that is ideally suited to an assembly-language subroutine. The following Basic program generates a series of 100 random integers (stored in A(0) to A(99)), and then sorts them by means of a "bubble" sort. (The bubble sort works by taking each value and comparing it to all remaining values to see if it is lower. If not, the values are exchanged and the process continues. In this way, the smallest values "float" to the top and larger ones to the bottom.) This program requires about a minute and a half of execution time in Basic (try it!). The numbers are printed first in unsorted order, and later in sorted order.

```
10 REM SORT 100 RANDOM INTEGERS
20 DEFINT A-Z: N=99: DIMA(N)
30 FOR I=0 TO N: A(I)=RND(1000): NEXT I
40 FOR I=0 TO N: PRINT I;A(I),: NEXT I
50 FOR I=0 TO N-1
```

```
 60 FOR J=I+1 TO N
 70 IF A(I)<=A(J) THEN 90
 80 X=A(I): A(I)=A(J): A(J)=X
 90 NEXT J,I
100 FOR I=0 TO N: PRINT I;A(I),: NEXT I
```

For this sort to be programmed in assembly language, we need the address of the A array and the value of N. It is an important aspect of the above program that N is a variable. N is set to 99 rather than 100 to make use of the A(0) variable. N can be changed to sort any number of random integers. We will poke the address of A into locations 7FFEH and 7FFFH (32766 and 32767), and pass N to the subroutine as the argument. The following Basic program sets up the sort and calls the subroutine, located at 7F00H. We must therefore set the memory size to 32515. This is a Level II subroutine. Disk Basic statements are indicated in remarks:

```
10 REM MACHINE LANGUAGE SORT
20 DEFINT A-Z: N=99: DIMA(N)
30 FOR I=0 TO N: A(I)=RND(1000): NEXT I
40 FOR I=0 TO N: PRINT I;A(I),: NEXT I
50 X=VARPTR(A(0)): POKE 32766,PEEK(VARPTR(X))
60 POKE 32767,PEEK(VARPTR(X)+1)
70 POKE 16526,0: POKE 16527,127
75 REM IN DISK BASIC, REPLACE 70 WITH DEFUSR0=&H7F00
80 X=USR(N): REM CALL SUBROUTINE
85 REM IN DISK BASIC, REPLACE 80 WITH X=USR0(N)
90 FOR I=0 TO N: PRINT I;A(I),: NEXT I
```

The subroutine that this program calls is shown below. This routine does exactly what the Basic program does and executes in less than one second. It will sort 1000 integers in about one minute.

```
        ORG     7F00H
ENTRY   CALL    0A7FH           ;put arg into HL
        PUSH    HL              ;HL=N
        POP     BC              ;transfer to BC
        LD      IX,(ADRA)       ;IX=address of A(I)
ILOOP   PUSH    BC              ;save outer loop index
        PUSH    IX
        POP     IY              ;IY=address of A(J)
JLOOP   INC     IY              ;A(I+1)
        INC     IY
        LD      H,(IX+1)        ;HL=A(I)
        LD      L,(IX)
        LD      D,(IY+1)        ;DE=A(J)
        LD      E,(IY)
        OR      A               ;clear carry
        SBC     HL,DE           ;A(I)-A(J)
```

```
             JR       Z,NEXTJ              ;=
             JR       C,NEXTJ              ;<
             ADC      HL,DE                ;restore HL
             LD       (IY+1),H             ;swap A(I)
             LD       (IY),L               ;with A(J)
             LD       (IX+1),D
             LD       (IX),E
NEXTJ        DEC      BC                   ;loop till BC=Ø
             LD       A,B
             OR       C
             JR       NZ,JLOOP
             POP      BC                   ;outer loop
             INC      IX                   ;next I
             INC      IX
             DEC      BC
             LD       A,B
             OR       C
             JR       NZ,ILOOP
             RET                           ;done!
             ORG      7FFEH
ADRA         DEFS     2
             END
```

This subroutine makes use of the fact that Level II Basic integers are standard 16-bit numbers that can be added or subtracted using the 16-bit arithmetic operations. Sorting other types of variables requires more complicated algorithms. The BC register pair is used to contain the index values for both the outer and inner loops. The value of the outer loop is saved in the stack while the inner loop is executed.

15.3 Alphabetizing a Series of Strings

Alphabetizing a series of strings is basically the same kind of problem as sorting a series of integers, except that the strings may be of different lengths. The following Basic program builds 100 random strings of 1 to 5 characters and then alphabetizes them. This process requires about two and a half minutes to execute in Basic:

```
10 REM SORT 100 RANDOM STRINGS
20 CLEAR 1000: DEFSTR A: DEFINT B-Z
30 N=99: DIMA(N)
40 FOR I=0 TO N: A(I)="" : REM INITIALIZE STRINGS
50 J=RND(5): FOR K=1 TO J: BUILD STRINGS OF 1-5 CHARS
60 A(I)=A(I)+CHR$(RND(26)+64)): NEXT K,I
70 FOR I=0 TO N: PRINT I;A(I),: NEXT I
80 FOR I=0 TO N-1: FOR J=I+1 TO N
90 IF A(I) <= A(J) THEN 110
100 X$=A(I): A(I)=A(J): A(J)=X$
```

```
110 NEXT J,I
120 FOR I=0 TO N: PRINT I; A(I),: NEXT I
```

To carry out the sorting function in assembly language, we
have to remember that, for string values, VARPTR(A$) returns
an address pointing to the LENGTH of the string, and the
ADDRESS of the string is in the next two bytes. The program
above can be revised as follows, to set up the call to a USR
subroutine to do the alphabetizing:

```
10 REM ALPHABETIZE STRINGS IN ASSEMBLY LANGUAGE
20 CLEAR 1000: DEFSTR A: DEFINT B-Z
30 N=99: DIM A(N)
40 FOR I=0 TO N: A(I)="": REM INITIALIZE STRINGS
50 J=RND(5): FOR K=1TO J: BUILD STRINGS OF 1-5 CHARS
60 A(I)=A(I)+CHR$(RND(26)+64): NEXT K,J
70 FOR I=0 TO N: PRINT I; A(I),: NEXT I
80 X=VARPTR(A(0)): POKE 32766,PEEK(VARPTR(X))
90 POKE 32767, PEEK(VARPTR(X)+1)
100 POKE 16526,0: POKE 16527,127
105 REM IN DISK BASIC REPLACE BY DEFUSR0=&H7F00
110 X=USR(N): REM IN DISK BASIC REPLACE BY X=USR0(N)
120 FOR I=0 TO N: PRINT I;A(I),: NEXT I
```

The assembly-language subroutine is as follows:

```
        ORG    7F00H
ENTRY   CALL   0A7FH          ;put n into HL
        PUSH   HL             ;move N to BC
        POP    BC
        LD     IX,(ADRA)      ;IX=VARPTR(A(I))
ILOOP   PUSH   BC             ;save I (outer loop)
        PUSH   IX
        POP    IY             ;IY=VARPTR(A(J))
JLOOP   PUSH   BC             ;save J (inner loop)
        INC    IY
        INC    IY
        INC    IY
        LD     B,(IX)         ;B=length of A(I)
        LD     C,(IY)         ;C=length of A(J)
        LD     L,(IX+1)       ;HL=address
        LD     H,(IX+2)       ;of A(I)
        LD     E,(IY+1)       ;DE=address
        LD     D,(IY+2)       ;of A(J)
COMP    LD     A,(DE)         ;A=char in A(J)
        CP     (HL)           ;compare to A(I)
        JR     C,SWAP         ;swap if <
        JR     NZ,NEXTJ       ;if NZ, continue
        INC    DE             ;try next char
        DEC    C              ;length of A(J)
        JR     Z,SWAP         ;if Z, no more chars
```

```
          INC      HL                 ;A(I)
          DJNZ     COMP
          JR       NEXTJ              ;if Z, order OK
SWAP      LD       B,(IX)             ;swap strings
          LD       L,(IX+1)           ;by changing
          LD       H,(IX+2)           ;pointers
          LD       C,(IY)
          LD       E,(IY+1)
          LD       D,(IY+2)
          LD       (IX),C
          LD       (IX+1),E
          LD       (IX+2),D
          LD       (IY),B
          LD       (IY+1),L
          LD       (IY+2),H
NEXTJ     POP      BC                 ;loop till
          DEC      BC                 ;BC=0
          LD       A,B
          OR       C
          JR       NZ,JLOOP
NEXTI     POP      BC                 ;outer loop
          INC      IX                 ;next I
          INC      IX
          INC      IX
          DEC      BC
          LD       A,B
          OR       C
          JR       NZ,ILOOP
          RET                         ;done!
ADRA      EQU      7FFEH
          END
```

    This subroutine alphabetizes 100 strings in about one
second, and 500 strings in about 25 seconds. Running the
program with the assembly-language subroutine shows that it
takes Basic much longer to build the random strings than it
does to alphabetize them. This is an excellent example of the
efficiency that can be achieved by using assembly-language
subroutines to do the tasks that they are ideally suited for.

16

DISK INPUT AND OUTPUT

This chapter is intended to provide basic information about the operation of the TRS-80's floppy disks. It covers the fundamentals and input-output operations, while chapter 17 presents details about the Disk Operating System and disk files. Much information about the disks is contained in Radio Shack's TRSDOS & DISK BASIC REFERENCE MANUAL. In addition, there are other books devoted exclusively to the disk, such as Harvard C. Pennington's TRS-80 DISK & OTHER MYSTERIES and William Barden's MICRO APPLICATIONS TRS-80 DISK INTERFACING GUIDE.

16.1 Disk Basics

The title of this section is "Disk Basics", not "Disk Basic". Basic is the main programming language of the TRS-80, and when you add a disk to the computer you have a large number of additional features available. Here we are covering preliminary information for the operation of the disk, and our discussion has nothing to do with the Basic language. In a sense, the TRS-80 is not a complete computer without a disk. Software to read the disk is contained in the ROM, and it is only when the configuration is tested and found not to contain a disk that Level II Basic is entered.

Everyone who owns a disk is familiar with the terms "tracks", "granules", and "sectors", but if you aren't familiar, then this information is new to you. The disk DRIVE is the piece of hardware into which a DISKETTE is inserted. The fact that the diskette can be removed is a vital aspect of its operation. The diskette is a round magnetic device similar to a phonograph record, except that information is recorded on it magnetically, and it is flexible or pliable and bends easily. It spins at approximately 300 RPM inside the paper wrapper in which it is kept. The magnetic impulses are read or written by a HEAD, which makes contact with the diskette through the oval-rectangular hole at the interior of the diskette. The diskette should always be handled carefully and replaced in its paper sleeve when not being used.

The surface of the diskette is divided into 35 concentric circles called TRACKS. (The fact that the inner tracks have a smaller surface area is of no concern to the operation of the system.) Each track is in turn divided into ten SECTORS. 256 bytes of data can be stored on each sector, and thus 2560 bytes on each track. The entire capacity of the diskette is 35 x 2560 = 89,600 bytes.

Other floppy disk systems may employ a different organization of the diskette, although the method used by Radio Shack is quite common. There are presently two kinds of floppy disk drives: eight-inch or standard disks and five-and-one-fourth inch or mini disks. The TRS-80 uses the mini disks, although the TRS-80 model II uses standard disks. The capacity of an 8-inch disk (over 500,000 bytes) is significantly greater than that of a mini disk.

Other disk systems may use 40 or 77 tracks on the diskette, and sometimes each track is divided into 16 sectors rather than ten. The TRS-80 uses SOFT-SECTORED diskettes, which means that there is only one little hole that must be sensed to find the beginning of the first sector on the diskette. The other sectors are found by sensing magnetic impulses that are written on the diskette when it is formatted. Formatting is something that you must do (by running a special program) to a new diskette before you use it the first time. Hard-sectored diskettes have either ten or 16 different holes that must be sensed by the disk controller.

16.2 The Disk Operating System

When you power up or "boot" a TRS-80 containing a disk, the computer expects that the diskette in the first drive, referred to as the "system" diskette in drive "zero", contains special information in the first sector of the first track. This track is part of a file called "BOOT/SYS", which contains a program that in turn reads much more information from the disk into memory. Only the first sector of this file is actually used for the bootstrap loader. Sectors 2-3 of the file contain an encoded copyright notice, which is displayed if you type "BOOT/SYS.WHO" and hold down the "2" and "6" keys simultaneously. Sectors 4-5 contain tables.

The program read into memory at power-on or reset is called the DISK OPERATING SYSTEM (DOS), and it is used for all disk input-output and some other functions. Radio Shack provides a DOS called TRSDOS, of which there have so far been four versions numbered 2.0 through 2.3. Several others are available from other companies. The most important of these are NEWDOS and NEWDOS80 available from Apparat, Inc.; and VTOS 3.0, available from Virtual Technology, Inc.

The DOS is organized into a series of "system" files referred to as SYS0 to SYS6, and some DOSs have file names up to SYS13. The reason for this organization is that there is not enough room in memory to have all functions available at all times, so the DOS automatically reads in what it needs when it needs it. The portion of memory used by the DOS extends approximately from locations 4200H through 5200H, and it is analogous to the ROM in that this information must not be disturbed by the programmer. Inclusion of the DOS on the system diskette takes up a significant portion of its 89K bytes, leaving only about 55K (46K when including BASIC and utilities) for user programs and data.

The main purpose of the DOS is that it allows you to refer to data on the disk as FILES rather than by tracks and sectors. A file contains as many sectors as it needs to contain, as long as they are all on the same diskette. It may be split up among various tracks all over the diskette, but you never have to worry about this even though you can refer to the individual sectors of the file. The DOS allocates space to the files in terms of GRANULES, consisting of five sectors or half a track each. A minimum of five sectors is allocated, even if you need only one. To keep the allocation of space straight, the DOS reserves track 17 (purposely in the middle of the diskette so that the head never has to move more than half its width) as a DIRECTORY track. This track contains the name of each file and all the information relating to its space allocation, and also tables called the HASH INDEX TABLE (HIT) and GRANULE ALLOCATION TABLE (GAT). These will be explained in Chapter 17.

While the organization of the disk into files does waste some of the space, it makes accessing the data on the disk very easy for the programmer. The DOS handles all of the input-output operations as well as the bookeeping.

     To understand how to use the disk, you need to know the
basic operations of the disk, which have nothing to do with
the file structure, and you also need to know how to use the
DOS, which is one of the most important aspects of the
computer.   Because Disk Basic spends much of its time
converting data into and out of strings, it is very slow and
inefficient in its use of disk input-output operations. The
true power of the disk can only be realized through
assembly-language programming.

                16.3   The Disk Controller

The heart of the TRS-80's disk system is the Western Digital
FD1771B-01 floppy disk controller chip, contained in the
expansion interface.   The disk drive used by Radio Shack is
the Shugart SA400. Many drives made by other companies have
also been used successfully, and are compatible with the
Shugart SA400. The disk controller chip is interfaced to the
TRS-80 by being directly connected to memory locations 37E0H
and 37ECH to 37EFH. This is to say that all disk input-output
operations are effected by storing or reading various bytes in
these locations.

     To read or write from the disk, you must first SELECT the
appropriate disk drive. This turns on the drive motor and
leaves it running for about three seconds. All subsequent
disk operations are directed to the drive selected. To select
a drive, a value specifying the drive must be stored in
location 37E0H (14304). The values 1, 2, 4, and 8 specify
drives 0, 1, 2, and 3, respectively.   The sequence of
operations:

                    LD   A,1
                    LD   (37E0H),A

selects drive zero.   Storing a value representing a
combination of these values, such as 3, which combines drives
0 and 1, selects two or more drives simultaneously, although
no standard software makes use of this feature (and it is
probably unreliable).

     The basic commands that may be issued to the disk
controller chip allow you to position the head and read or
write data. The basic commands are as follows:

          1.   Restore: move the head to track zero.
          2.   Seek: find the currently specified track.
          3.   Step: step the head in the last direction.
          4.   Step In: step the head one track in.
          5.   Step Out: step the head one track out.

6. Read: read one byte of data.
7. Write: write one byte of data.
8. Read Address: read ID field.
9. Read Track: read entire track.
10. Write Track: write entire track.
11. Force Interrupt: terminate operation.

The disk controller contains various registers and status indicators. Location 37ECH (14316) is the COMMAND register. Most disk operations are accomplished by loading the proper value into this location, once a drive has been selected. Another is the STATUS register, which is used to test whether a previous operation has been completed and whether the disk is ready for another command or for data. The status register is read by reading location 37ECH, the same as the command register. 37EFH (14319) is the DATA register. Data is read from the diskette in serial order, and always passed into or out of this location in quantities of one byte. The data register is also used to hold various other values when commands are issued. Other registers include the TRACK register, which is at location 37EDH (14317), and the SECTOR register, at location 37EEH (14318). They hold information about the track and sector currently being used.

Most disk commands are executed by simply storing a particular value into location 37ECH. The following table shows the values that must be loaded in order to accomplish the functions indicated:

Value	Function	Value	Function
03H	restore	A8H	write data byte
13H	seek	A9H	write byte on
33H	step last		directory track
	direction	C2H	read address
53H	step in	E4H	read track
73H	step out	F4H	write track
88H	read byte	D0H	force interrupt

To be sure, other values may be used to perform these same functions with minor differences in operation, but these are the values normally used for these operations on the TRS-80.

When data is read or written from a disk, the cpu must continually be ready to respond to the disk controller. All other operations must be locked out. Interrupts must be disabled, and the cpu must be in a loop, testing the status of the controller. Since disk operations are usually very fast, this is a minimum amount of overhead, but it does mean that the TRS-80 cannot be used in certain real-time applications where it must be ready to respond to external conditions.

One other point about the disk system is that the presence of the write protect tab does nothing but set a bit in the status register. The protection of data on write-protected diskettes is entirely a function of the software.

16.4 Disk Operations

After selecting the drive, the first operation we might want to perform might be a restore, which moves the head to track zero. This is accomplished by storing the value 3 in location 37ECH (14316). We must then test the value in 37EC to determine whether the disk has completed its operation. When bit zero of this location goes to zero, the operation is finished and the head is positioned over track zero. As long as it remains a one, we must wait before performing any further disk operation.

One way of locating any track on the disk is to move the head to track zero, and then step in until the desired track is found. The step-in operation is done by storing the value 53H (83) in location 37ECH. Conversely, stepping out is performed by storing the value 73H (115) in 37EC, and stepping from the last direction by storing 33H (51) in the same location. After performing a step operation, we again must test the status of the disk and wait until the operation is complete. To verify what track the head is currently positioned over, we can read the track register by simply loading the contents of location 37EDH (14317).

A better way of finding a particular track is to use the seek command, which automatically positions the head to a specified track. To use this command, the track number (0 to 34) must first be loaded into location 37EFH (14319), after the drive has been selected. The sector can also be specified by storing the sector number in 37EEH (14318). Seek is then executed by storing 1BH (27) into location 37ECH.

All of the above head-positioning operations may be accomplished in Basic, by simply POKEing and PEEKing into the proper locations. The following Basic program selects drive zero, restores it to track zero, and then asks you to specify a track number. The head is then positioned over this track by means of the seek command, and the track number is read from the track register and printed, to verify that the proper track has been located. Then the program returns and asks you for a new track. The subroutine at statement 150 tests the status of the last operation and waits until it has been completed.

```
 10 POKE 14304,1                      select drive zero
 20 POKE 14316,3                      restore to track zero
 30 GOSUB 150                         wait until done
 40 INPUT"TRACK #";T                  get track #
 50 POKE 14304,1                      select again
 60 POKE 14319,T                      output track #
 70 GOSUB 150                         wait
 80 POKE 14316,19                     seek
 90 GOSUB 150                         wait
100 A=PEEK(14317)                     read track register
110 PRINT A                           print it
120 A=PEEK(14316)                     get status
130 PRINT A                           print status
140 GOTO 40                           try another track
150 A=PEEK(14316)                     test status
160 IF (A AND 1) <> 0 THEN 150        loop if busy
170 RETURN                            done
```

One impression you may have when running this program is
that the disk finds the proper track almost immediately, and
if you do not input a new track number within three seconds,
the drive motor is turned off. It is true that the head can
be positioned over any track in no more than a couple of
seconds, but this speed is nothing when compared to the rate
at which data is read or written from the disk. The latter is
so fast that it cannot be done in Basic at all.

Reading and writing of data on the disk is normally done
with only the read and write byte commands, on a single sector
at a time. The read track, write track, and read address
commands are usually used only in formatting the disk, but it
is possible to read and write entire tracks of data. The read
and write byte commands can also read and write multiple
sectors (from 2 to 9), although this feature is almost never
used. Finally, note that the directory track must be written
with a different code, although it can be read as any track.
This property is used to protect the status of the directory
track, without which the DOS cannot function, as well as to
distinguish the directory from the other tracks.

Reading or writing data can only be done after a sequence
of operations such as shown above has been executed. Once the
disk has been selected and head positioned, the status must be
continuously tested. When it indicates that a byte is ready
to be read from the data register, the byte must be taken and
stored in the buffer immediately, and the process repeated
until the entire sector or track has been read.

To illustrate how this works, let us examine the portion of
the ROM that reads the "BOOT" file from the system drive into
memory. BOOT itself is a "bootstrap loader", which loads in

the rest of the DOS once it is entered. This program starts
at location Ø696H in the ROM. What follows is a disassembled
listing of the ROM to which comments have been appended:

```
Ø696        LD      A,(37ECH)           ;test
Ø699        INC     A                   ;disk
Ø69A        CP      2                   ;status
Ø69C        JP      C,ØØ75H             ;go to Level II if no disk
Ø69F        LD      A,1                 ;drive zero
Ø6A1        LD      (37E1H),A           ;select it
Ø6A4        LD      HL,37ECH            ;command and status address
Ø6A7        LD      DE,37EFH            ;data address
Ø6AA        LD      (HL),3              ;restore command
Ø6AC        LD      BC,Ø                ;delay 64K times
Ø6AF        CALL    60H                 ;ROM delay routine
Ø6B2        BIT     Ø,(HL)              ;test status
Ø6B4        JR      NZ,Ø6B2H            ;wait if busy
Ø6B6        XOR     A                   ;zero A
Ø6B7        LD      (37EEH),A           ;select sector Ø
Ø6BA        LD      BC,4200H            ;where to put data
Ø6BD        LD      A,8CH               ;read command
Ø6BF        LD      (HL),A              ;read sector zero
Ø6CØ        BIT     1,(HL)              ;test status
Ø6C2        JR      Z,Ø6CØH             ;wait until ready
Ø6C4        LD      A,(DE)              ;read byte
Ø6C5        LD      (BC),A              ;store in 4200H ff
Ø6C6        INC     C                   ;increment pointer
Ø6C7        JR      NZ,Ø6CØH            ;continue until 256 bytes read
Ø6C9        JP      4200H               ;jump to DOS bootstrap loader
```

     This listing illustrates many aspects of how disk input and
output programming works. The double registers BC, DE, and HL
are always loaded with addresses that are used in fetching and
storing data, because instructions like "LD A,(HL)" are faster
to execute than "LD A,(37EFH)", and the address can be changed
by an INC instruction.   In this example, "INC C" is used
rather than "INC BC" because it sets the condition codes and
only 256 bytes are being read.

                16.5 Disk Input/Output Subroutines

We now have enough information to write generalized disk read
and write subroutines. At this point it is necessary to
mention that all TRSDOS routines have curious time-wasting
instructions such as:

```
                PUSH    AF
                POP     AF
```

after various disk operations are performed. Presumably these

are included either because of undocumented problems with   the
disk controller chip, or as a precaution.

   The following subroutine reads a single sector from the
diskette in drive zero. The track and sector is specified in
the DE register pair, D indicating the track and E the sector,
and the buffer where incoming data is to be stored is in BC.
The "AND 5CH" tests for various errors that may occur during
the   operation, and terminates it by a force interrupt
instruction if an error occurs.

```
RDSECT  DI                              ;disable interrupts
        LD      A,1                     ;drive zero
        LD      (37E0H),A               ;select
        PUSH    BC                      ;save BC
        LD      BC,0                    ;wait 64K times
        CALL    60H                     ;ROM delay subroutine
        POP     BC                      ;restore BC
        LD      HL,37ECH                ;command register address
        LD      A,1                     ;select again
        LD      (37E0H),A
        LD      (37EEH),DE              ;specify track & sector
        LD      (HL),13H                ;seek
        PUSH    BC                      ;waste time
        POP     BC
        PUSH    BC                      ;waste more time
        POP     BC
WAIT    LD      A,(HL)                  ;get status
        RRCA                            ;busy bit to carry
        JR      C,WAIT                  ;wait until done
DSKCM   LD      (HL),88H                ;read byte command
        LD      DE,37EFH                ;data register
        JR      RDLOOP                  ;start reading
BUSY    RRCA                            ;busy bit to carry
        JR      NC,TSTERR               ;if not busy
RDLOOP  LD      A,(HL)                  ;get status
        BIT     1,A                     ;test
        JR      Z,BUSY                  ;wait if busy
DSKIO   LD      A,(DE)                  ;get byte
        LD      (BC),A                  ;store in buffer
        INC     BC                      ;increment pointer
        JR      RDLOOP                  ;continue
TSTERR  LD      A,(HL)                  ;get status
        AND     5CH                     ;test errors
        RET     Z                       ;done if no errors
        LD      (HL),0D0H               ;force interrupt
        CALL    ERRMSG                  ;print error message
        RET                             ;done
```

   Disk write subroutines are handled in much the same way,
except that the data register must first be loaded with a byte

and the status then checked to determine if the controller   is
ready for the next byte. In fact, exactly the same subroutine
as above could be used if the instruction at DSKCM is   changed
to:

```
        LD      (HL),ØA8H          ;write byte
```

and the two instructions at DSKIO are changed to:

```
        LD      A,(BC)             ;get byte
        LD      (DE),A             ;store in data register
```

It   must   be   understood   that   this   discussion   is   an
oversimplification of the entire process, although it does
serve to provide information that will be satisfactory for
most purposes.

16.6 TRSDOS Input-Output Subroutines

There is little reason to include much information about the
TRSDOS input-output subroutines, because this information is
covered well and in detail in Radio Shack's TRSDOS & DISK
BASIC REFERENCE MANUAL.   All known DOSs use the   same
subroutine calls.

File handling is controlled through a data control block or
DCB. Before the file is opened, the DCB contains the complete
name of the file (including the extension, password, and drive
number).   When the DCB is open, other information is stored
there. When open, the most important items in the DCB are the
EOF (offset of last delimited in last record), LRL (logical
record length), NRN (next record number to read or write) and
ERN (ending record number). These are located at DCB bytes 8,
9, 1Ø-11, and 12-13, respectively.

One of the basic ideas behind these subroutines is that, by
setting the logical record length when opening the file and
POSN to position it, records of any length (up to 256 bytes)
may be read or written. The DOS takes care of any problems
arising from the fact that these records may span two sectors
in the file. Recent DOSs such as VTOS 3.Ø and NEWDOS8Ø
incorporate this feature in Basic programming. With other
DOSs, it can only be accessed through assembly-language
programming.   In most cases, an entire sector is read or
written at one time. LRL is set to zero for this purpose.

All TRSDOS subroutines require that the address of the DCB
be loaded into the DE register pair before the system call is
made, and the zero flag is set on exit to indicate whether the
operation was successful. If there was an error (i.e., if NZ

was set), A contains the error code. Other calling parameters are noted for the individual subroutines, which are as follows:

Name	Address	Function	Calling Parameters
INIT	4420H	Create file if none exists.	HL => buffer B = LRL
OPEN	4424H	Open existing file.	Same as for INIT
POSN	4442H	Position file, if LRL <>0	BC = logical record number
READ	4436H	Read record.	HL => UREC if LRL<>0
WRITE	4439H	Write record.	Same as for READ
VERF	443CH	Write record with verify.	Same as for READ
CLOSE	4428H	Close file.	
KILL	442CH	Kill file.	

While the information in the manual is mostly complete, the following errors and incompatibilities should be noted:

ERN contains the last record number when a file is opened. Following a write operation, it contains the number of the record just written. When writing a record into the middle of a file, ERN must be fixed before the file is closed.

The error message subroutine at 4409H sometimes prints messages of an incorrect length, producing a message that scrolls off the video display before you can read it. It is best simply to print the error number, or to include error-recovery procedures in user programs.

There is a major incompatibility between all versions of TRSDOS and NEWDOS and NEWDOS80 concerning the way in which the EOF, ERN and NRN parameters in the DCB are maintained. When operating under NEWDOS or NEWDOS80, ERN contains the ending record number only when the EOF is on a sector boundary. These details are described in Apparat's "ZAP" documentation, which gives a list of corrections for NEWDOS version 2.1., and in the NEWDOS80 documentation.

17

DISK FILES

17.1 The Disk Directory

The disk directory, normally placed on track 17 unless that track is locked out, is the key to understanding the entire file structure on the diskette. Unfortunately, Radio Shack has never released many details about these technical matters, but much useful information is contained in the documentation for Apparat's NEWDOS and NEWDOS80, and in H.C. Pennington's TRS-80 DISK & OTHER MYSTERIES.

The first two sectors of the directory track contain the Granule Allocation Table (GAT) and Hash Index Table (HIT). The remaining eight tracks contain directory entries, either primary entries ("FPDE" for "File Primary Directory Entry") or extension entries ("FXDE" for "File Extension Directory Entry"). Each entry is 32 bytes long. There is thus a maximum of eight entries per sector and 64 entries (which may mean less than 64 files) on the diskette. (Why the DOS allows a maximum of 50 files on a formatted diskette and 60 on a system diskette is unknown.) All of this data is quite straightforward to interpret if you know how.

146

17.2 The GAT Sector

The GAT sector contains two tables indicating the space
available for files on the disk and whether any tracks are
locked out.   In addition, it contains the hash code for the
diskette's password, the diskette name and date, and the AUTO
command file that is to be called on power on or reset.   All
passwords are encoded in a "hash code" explained below (see
section 17.6).

The first 96 bytes of the GAT sector (bytes 00 to 5FH)
contain the Granule Allocation Table itself.   Since the Radio
Shack disk drives use only 35 tracks, only the first 35 bytes
(00 to 22H) are actually used, although the DOS contains
provision for expansion up to 96 tracks on the disk.   Each
byte simply indicates whether one or both granules on the
track is free or already allocated to a file, according to the
following table:

binary	hexadecimal	meaning
11111100	FC	both granules (sectors 0-9) free
11111101	FD	only first granule (sectors 0-4) allocated
11111110	FE	only second granule (sectors 5-9) allocated
11111111	FF	both granules (sectors 0-9) allocated

The next 96 bytes contain the Track Lock Out Table.   This
table is exactly the same as the GAT, only its function is to
tell the DOS whether a track can be used at all.   The purpose
of these tables is to make it simple for the DOS to know how
much space it has available and where the space is.

Why would a track be locked out?   There are several
reasons.   It can be locked out because the track could not be
verified during a FORMAT or BACKUP operation.   You may also
want to use special software, such as that described in
Chapter 16, to write certain tracks and therefore not make
them available for the DOS.

The final 64 bytes of the GAT sector contain a variety of
miscellaneous information.   The password hash code is in bytes
CE-CFH.   The diskette name and date are in bytes D0 to DF;
each of these requires exactly eight bytes.   Finally, the AUTO
command file is in E0-FF, indicated simply as a command
followed by a carriage return.   The absence of a command is
indicated by placing a carriage return in byte E0.   The
remaining bytes are filled with FF.   A map of the entire GAT
sector is shown below.

"GAT" Sector Map (Track 17, sector 0)

```
        0  1  2  3  4  5  6  7  8  9  A  B  C  D  E  F
   00   <-----------GRANULE ALLOCATION TABLE-----------
   10   -----------------------------------------------
   20   ------->
   30                        (unused)
   40                        (unused)
   50                        (unused)
   60   <-------------TRACK LOCK OUT TABLE-------------
   70   -----------------------------------------------
   80   ------->
   90                        (unused)
   A0                        (unused)
   B0                        (unused)
   C0   <---------------(UNKNOWN)---------------><PSW>
   D0   <-----------DISKETTE NAME AND DATE-----------> 
   E0   <------------"AUTO" COMMAND FILE-------------- 
   F0   ----------------------------------------------->
```

17.3   The "HIT" Sector

The HIT sector (sector 1 of the directory track) contains
information concerning each file name in the directory.   Only
the first eight bytes of each 32-byte segment of the sector
are used. Each file name in the directory has a single byte
of hash code in the table. The POSITION of the byte in the
table relates to its address in the direktory.   The last
hexadecimal digit (0-7) plus 2 gives the sector number in the
directory track where the file entry is stored, and the first
digit (only even values from 0 to E) times 16 gives the
relative byte where the entry starts within the sector.   The
following map shows the correspondence between the HIT sector
and the directory entries:

```
        0    1    2    3    4    5    6    7     + 2 = sector
   00  200  300  400  500  600  700  800  900    (bytes 8-F unused)
   20  220  320  420  520  620  720  820  920
   40  240  340  440  540  640  740  840  940
   60  260  360  460  560  660  760  860  960
   80  280  380  480  580  680  780  880  980
   A0  2A0  3A0  4A0  5A0  6A0  7A0  8A0  9A0
   C0  2C0  3C0  4C0  5C0  6C0  7C0  8C0  9C0
   E0  2E0  3E0  4E0  5E0  6E0  7E0  8E0  9E0
```

*16 = byte

In this map, a number like "280" means "sector 2, byte 80H" of
the directory track.   Each directory entry is 32 bytes long.

If you look at a listing of a HIT sector for a particular
diskette, you may notice that some of the codes for different
files are identical. This is perfectly normal, and simply
means that the number produced must correspond to the code
derived from the name of the file. It does not mean that all
codes must be unique. The purpose of the HIT sector is to
tell the DOS where active entries are located within the
directory, and then to verify that these entries correspond to
the files specified. A zero in the HIT byte means that no
entry is stored in the directory.

17.4 File Primary Directory Entries (FPDEs)

The bulk of the directory track, sectors 2-9, is reserved for
file entries. Almost all of these are FILE PRIMARY DIRECTORY
ENTRIES or FPDEs. A FILE EXTENSION DIRECTORY ENTRY or FXDE
occurs only when a particular file is not only very large, but
also split among more than four separate extents. In the
remaining discussion we will refer to directory entries by
their shorthand names, FPDEs or FXDEs.

Each FPDE or FXDE is 32 bytes long, the same as the TRSDOS
DCBs. The purpose of the FPDE is to provide information on
the name of the file, what type of file it is, whether it has
update or access passwords, and where it is located. The FXDE
gives additional information on where the file is located.
Since space is always allocated in terms of granules, this is
the most complicated aspect of the entries.

The way space allocation works is as follows: when the DOS
allocates a granule to the file, it checks to see that this is
the first free granule following used space. As sectors are
added to the file, additional granules are allocated following
the first one, until a sector is encountered that is being
used by another active file. At this point the DOS issues
another extent to the file, which begins with another granule
on a completely different track and sector. The more files
that are added to a diskette, the more complicated the space
allocation becomes. It is quite common for files to have
several extents on different tracks, jumping all about the
diskette. There is room for four extents in the FPDE and four
more in each additional FXDE.

The information in the FPDE is quite specific, and can be
summarized in tabular form:

Byte (hex)	Meaning
Ø	File Type: Bit 7: Ø=FPDE, 1=FXDE
	Bit 6: 1=system file, Ø=non-system file
	Bit 5: unused
	Bit 4: 1=file exists in HIT sector, Ø = file killed
	Bit 3: 1=invisible file, Ø=visible
	Bits Ø-2: protection level, according to the following code:
	(111 binary=) 7 = no access
	6 = execution access only
	5 = read and execute only
	4 = write, read, execute
	3 = (unused)
	2 = rename, write, read, execute
	1 = kill, rename, write, read, execute
	Ø = no restrictions
1-2	Unused by FPDE.
3	End of File (EOF) byte: last byte used in last sector of the file.
4	Logical Record Length (LRL): this concept is used only by VTOS 3.Ø and NEWDOS8Ø.
5-C	File Name: 8 characters, padded with blanks on the right if necessary.
D-F	Extension: 3 characters, padded with blanks as name.
1Ø-11	Update Password, stored as 2-byte hash code.
12-13	Access password, stored as 2-byte hash code.
14-15	EOF Relative Sector: if the EOF byte (3) contains zero, then this byte is the relative sector count of the file; but if byte 3 is non-zero, then it contains the relative count plus one. Since a file may contain more than 256 sectors, this entry is a two-byte word, stored in reverse (LSB/MSB).
16-1F	Five 2-byte pairs specifying EXTENTS:
	1st byte: if FF (255), signifies end of extents.
	if FE (254), then 2nd byte contains a DIRECTORY ENTRY CODE (DEC) pointing to an FXDE that contains additional extent information.
	if Ø-22 (Ø-34), TRACK NUMBER on diskette where this entry starts.
	2nd byte (if 1st byte <254):
	bits 5-7: number of granules from start of track to start of eptent (Ø or 1).
	bits Ø-4: number (-1) of contiguous granules assigned to this extent.

The first byte of the file extent is easy to read. It is simply the track number. The second byte must be broken down into bits, but the following simple rules apply:

     1. If this byte is Ø-19H, the extent starts at sector zero.

     2. If it is 20H or greater, the extent starts at sector five. In this case, subtracting 20H from the value in this byte will give you the granule count.

Let us clarify the extent bytes with some examples:

(a) 12 ØØ   The extent begins on track 12H (18), sector zero. One granule is assigned to the extent.

(b) Ø5 21   The extent begins on track 5, sector 5. Two granules are assigned to this extent.

(c) 15 23   The extent begins on track 15H (21), sector 5. Four granules are assigned to the extent.

(d) 13 30   The extent begins on track 13H (19), sector 5. 17 granules are assigned to this extent.

17.5 File Extension Directory Entries (FXDEs)

FXDEs contain only information about file extents, and a pointer to the FPDE. All remaining data about the file is in the FPDE. The bytes used by the FXDE are as follows:

Byte	Meaning
Ø	> 80H (Bit 7=1 for FXDE)
1	DEC to FPDE (see below)
2-15	unused, and should contain zeros.
16-1F	Extents, same as in FPDE.

If byte 30 of the FPDE contains the value FE (254), then byte 31 contains a DIRECTORY ENTRY CODE (DEC) pointing to the FXDE. Similarly, byte 1 of the FXDE contains a DEC pointing back to the FPDE. If you recall the information about the HIT sector, all directory entries are stored in 32-byte blocks in sectors 2-9 of the directory track. The DEC byte is decoded as follows:

Bits Ø-2 + 2 = the sector containing the FXDE (or FPDE).
Bits 3-4: unused.
Bits 5-7 = the number of the entry within the sector.
               (There are 8 32-byte entries in each sector, numbered Ø-7.)

The following examples may help clarify how to decode
DECs:

	Hex	Binary	Meaning
(a)	40H =	010 00 000	sector 2, entry 2 (the THIRD entry, starting from 0). This entry is in bytes 40-5FH (64-95) of the sector.
(b)	A6H =	101 00 110	sector 8, entry 5, stored in bytes A0-BFH (160-191).
(c)	83H =	100 00 011	sector 5, entry 4, stored in bytes 80-9FH (128-159).

17.6 Passwords and Hash Codes

"Hash code" is a term describing the process for taking a
character string and converting it into an encoded value.
Each byte of the string is multiplied by some value. The
codes are then added together to produce the hash. Different
strings may produce the same values, and there are hundreds of
different hashing methods.

All passwords stored in the directory track are stored in
hash code, so that you cannot simply read the sectors and find
out what they are. If you want to read a file that is
protected by a password that you don't know, the easiest
procedure is to modify the diskette directory so that it
contains a password that you do know. The password for a
string of all blanks, indicating no password, is 96 42. Both
the SUPERZAP and MON4 programs contain procedures for
modifying disk sectors independent of the file structure.

If you want to find out the hash code for a particular
password, you need to know the formula used by Radio Shack.
The password, a string of 8 bytes padded with blanks on the
right, is operated on according to the polynomial

$$X**16 + X**12 + X**5 + 1$$

and the numerical result is the two-byte hash code. The
following program allows you to input a password or exactly
eight bytes (no backspacing permitted!), and then displays the
hash code:

```
        ORG     7000H
START   CALL    01C9H    ;clear screen
        LD      A,14     ;cursor on
        CALL    33H
```

```
NEXT     LD      A,'?'               ;print prompt
         CALL    33H
         LD      HL,PASSWD           ;buffer
         LD      B,8                 ;8 bytes
INPUT    CALL    49H                 ;input string
         LD      (HL),A
         CALL    33H                 ;display
         INC     HL
         DJNZ    INPUT
         CALL    CR                  ;print carriage return
         LD      HL,PASSWD+7
         LD      DE,1E0CH            ;initial code
         LD      C,8                 ;8 characters
         JR      L4
L1       LD      B,8
L2       RR      D
         RR      E
         JR      NC,L3
         LD      A,10H
         XOR     E
         LD      E,A
         LD      A,88H
         XOR     D
         LD      D,A
L3       DJNZ    L2
L4       LD      A,D
         XOR     (HL)
         LD      D,A
         DEC     HL
         DEC     C
         JR      NZ,L1
         EX      DE,HL               ;result to HL
         LD      A,L                 ;print in
         CALL    HEX                 ;reverse order
         LD      A,H
         CALL    HEX
         CALL    CR                  ;print carriage return
         JR      NEXT                ;get another password
CR       LD      A,13
         JP      33H
HEX      PUSH    AF                  ;print A in hex
         RRCA
         RRCA
         RRCA
         RRCA
         CALL    HEX2
         POP     AF
HEX2     AND     15
         ADD     A,30H
         CP      3AH
         JP      C,33H
```

```
          ADD      A,7
          JP       33H
PASSWD    DEFS     8
          END      START
```

This program does not provide a formula for discovering the password corresponding to a particular hash code, but lets you experiment to find a specific value. This is the method used for TRSDOS 2.1 and 2.2, but it has been modified for 2.3. The following table shows all the known hash codes and passwords used by TRSDOS 2.1, 2.2 and 2.3, NEWDOS 2.1, and VTOS 3.0:

Hash Code	Password(s)	Used by
1FB2	'BGBI '	Access for BOOT/SYS, all DOSs
210E	'AJJJ '	Access for system files, all DOSs
2A5F	'BGBQ '	Access for VTOS 3.0 FORMAT, BACKUP, etc.
607F	'EQFY '	Update for BOOT/SYS, all DOSs
782F	'BASIC '	Update for TRSDOS 2.2 & 2.3 BASIC, BASICR
8130	'RVCOOK '	TRSDOS 2.1 & NEWDOS FORMAT, COPY, BASIC, BACKUP
9642	' '	ALL files with no password
982F	'FORMAT '	Update for TRSDOS 2.2 & 2.3 FORMAT
A261	'F3GUM ' 'NV36 '	TRSDOS 2.1 system files
A71D	'DNRU '	Update for DIR/SYS, all DOSs
ACA8	'BACKUP '	Update for TRSDOS 2.2 & 2.3 BACKUP
DD61	'LOY4 '	TRSDOS 2.2 & 2.3 system files
E042	'PASSWORD'	Disk password, all DOSs
EB29	'XNTR '	Update for system files, all DOSs
F9E5	'DLSD '	Access for DIR/SYS, all DOSs

17.7 File Structures and Types

Several different types of files are stored on diskettes: Basic program files, object program files, system files, and data files. Special types of files include Editor/Assembler source files and Electric Pencil data files. File types are usually indicated by the extension part of the file name (following the "/"). It is always a good idea for you to use extensions even though they cause more typing. Standard extensions are "BAS" for Basic programs, "CMD" for object programs, "DAT" for data files, "SYS" for system files, "ASM" or "SOR" for Editor/Assembler source files, and "PCL" for Electric Pencil files.

Files are simply blocks of 256 bytes, stored in successive sectors of the diskette. The system software ALWAYS writes 256 bytes at a time, meaning that it writes whatever garbage is left in memory in the last sector following the last byte that you use. Another important point is that all standard file types use 256-byte records, although Basic programs are able to read only 255 bytes because of the limitations on the size of Basic strings.

(A) ASCII Basic Program Files

Files stored in this form appear exactly as they were entered into memory. LISTing the program under the DOS produces the same listing as under Basic. Each line begins with a line number, followed by a space and the program text, terminating in a carriage return. Loading files stored in this form takes longer, because each line must undergo a translation process just as when you type it in. One advantage of ASCII Basic program files is that they can be read and edited by the Electric Pencil.

(B) Binary Basic Program Files

Most Basic programs are stored in this form, which is actually a dump of the way in which the program is stored in memory during execution. Line numbers are stored in two bytes, and each Basic key word is translated into its binary "token". Other items, such as variable names and strings, are not translated. The very first byte of the file is FFH (255). Following that byte, individual lines are encoded as units according to the following scheme:

```
bytes 1-2:  pointer to NEXT line number in memory
bytes 3-4:  line number, in binary (LSB/MSB)
bytes 5-n:  program text (n=last byte of text)
byte  n+1:  zero.
```

The end of the program is recognized by zeros in bytes 1-2 of the line code. When combined with zero at the end of the previous line, they produce a series of three successive zeros.

(C) Object Program Files

Object program or command files are produced by the Editor/Assembler program, or transferred to the disk by the TAPEDISK utility or some other program like MON4. An object program is executable machine code. All that is necessary is

for it to be read into the proper locations, and then for
control to be transferred to the starting address. (For this
reason, object programs must not be read into the portion of
RAM occupied by the DOS, for the DOS will be bombed.)

Object programs are loaded in blocks which have the
following format:

```
byte 1:    code for function of bytes in block:
           01 = load into address specified
           02 = entry point address
           any other value = do not load this block
                   (it contains comments only)
byte 2:    byte count (usually 80H or less)
bytes 3-4: address where block loaded or control
           transferred to
bytes 5-n: data (unused if byte 1=2)
byte n+1:  checksum for block
```

The transfer address must be the last block in the file.
If you do not specify an address to the Editor/Assembler
program, this value defaults to zero.

(D) System Files

System files, including SYS0 to SYSn as well as BOOT/SYS
and DIR/SYS, have exactly the same format as object program
files. (DIR/SYS has a different structure discussed in detail
above.) All system files on standard diskettes have an
extensive copyright notice at the beginning.

(E) Editor/Assembler Source Files

Source files to the disk version of the Editor/Assembler
program (available on NEWDOS) use the same format as source
tapes. Each line is stored as a separate short block. The
complete format is as follows:

```
byte 1 (of file):  D3H
bytes 2-7:  file name, stored as succession
            of six characters padded with blanks.
            Do not rename EDTASM files!
bytes 1-5 (of block):  line number, ASCII with bit 7
            set (80H added to ASCII value).
byte 6:  blank space (20H)
bytes 7-n:  complete line statement, terminating with
            carriage return (0DH). Right arrow TAB
            key stored as 09H.
last byte of file:  1AH (end-of-file byte)
```

(F)   Electric Pencil Files

These files are simply a string of ASCII characters with no
special codes. Each record terminates with a carriage return,
and the end of the file is signified by the EOF byte 00.

(G)   Data Files

Data files have no set rules for their structure. You make
the rules when you write the data and read it back, or when
you use the FIELD statement in Basic.

APPENDIX A: Zilog Tables of Z-80 Instructions

The following section gives a summary of the Z-80 instruction
set.   The instructions are logically arranged into groups as
shown in tables 7.0-1 through 7.0-11. Each table shows the
assembly-language mnemonic OP code, the actual OP code, the
symbolic operation, the content of the flag register following
the execution of each instruction, the number of bytes
required for each instruction, as well as the number of memory
cycles and the total number of T states (external clock
periods) required for the fetching and execution of each
instruction.

Mnemonic	Symbolic Operation	Flags						OP-Code	No. of Bytes	No. of M Cycles	No. of T Cycles	Comments	
		C	Z	P/V	S	N	H	76 543 210					
LD r, r′	r ← r′	•	•	•	•	•	•	01 r r′	1	1	4	r, r′	Reg.
LD r, n	r ← n	•	•	•	•	•	•	00 r 110	2	2	7	000	B
								← n →				001	C
LD r, (HL)	r ← (HL)	•	•	•	•	•	•	01 r 110	1	2	7	010	D
LD r, (IX+d)	r ← (IX+d)	•	•	•	•	•	•	11 011 101	3	5	19	011	E
								01 r 110				100	H
								← d →				101	L
LD r, (IY+d)	r ← (IY+d)	•	•	•	•	•	•	11 111 101	3	5	19	111	A
								01 r 110					
								← d →					
LD (HL), r	(HL) ← r	•	•	•	•	•	•	01 110 r	1	2	7		
LD (IX+d), r	(IX+d) ← r	•	•	•	•	•	•	11 011 101	3	5	19		
								01 110 r					
								← d →					
LD (IY+d), r	(IY+d) ← r	•	•	•	•	•	•	11 111 101	3	5	19		
								01 110 r					
								← d →					
LD (HL), n	(HL) ← n	•	•	•	•	•	•	00 110 110	2	3	10		
								← n →					
LD (IX+d), n	(IX+d) ← n	•	•	•	•	•	•	11 011 101	4	5	19		
								00 110 110					
								← d →					
								← n →					
LD (IY+d), n	(IY+d) ← n	•	•	•	•	•	•	11 111 101	4	5	19		
								00 110 110					
								← d →					
								← n →					
LD A, (BC)	A ← (BC)	•	•	•	•	•	•	00 001 010	1	2	7		
LD A, (DE)	A ← (DE)	•	•	•	•	•	•	00 011 010	1	2	7		
LD A, (nn)	A ← (nn)	•	•	•	•	•	•	00 111 010	3	4	13		
								← n →					
								← n →					
LD (BC), A	(BC) ← A	•	•	•	•	•	•	00 000 010	1	2	7		
LD (DE), A	(DE) ← A	•	•	•	•	•	•	00 010 010	1	2	7		
LD (nn), A	(nn) ← A	•	•	•	•	•	•	00 110 010	3	4	13		
								← n →					
								← n →					
LD A, I	A ← I	•	‡	IFF	‡	0	0	11 101 101	2	2	9		
								01 010 111					
LD A, R	A ← R	•	‡	IFF	‡	0	0	11 101 101	2	2	9		
								01 011 111					
LD I, A	I ← A	•	•	•	•	•	•	11 101 101	2	2	9		
								01 000 111					
LD R, A	R ← A	•	•	•	•	•	•	11 101 101	2	2	9		
								01 001 111					

Notes: r, r′ means any of the registers A, B, C, D, E, H, L

IFF   the content of the interrupt enable flip-flop (IFF) is copied into the P/V flag

Flag Notation: • = flag not affected, 0 = flag reset, 1 = flag set, X = flag is unknown,

‡ = flag is affected according to the result of the operation.

8-BIT LOAD GROUP

Mnemonic	Symbolic Operation	Flags						Op-Code 76 543 210	No. of Bytes	No. of M Cycles	No. of T States	Comments
		C	Z	P/V	S	N	H					
LD dd, nn	dd ← nn	●	●	●	●	●	●	00 dd0 001 ← n → ← n →	3	3	10	dd Pair 00 BC 01 DE
LD IX, nn	IX ← nn	●	●	●	●	●	●	11 011 101 00 100 001 ← n → ← n →	4	4	14	10 HL 11 SP
LD IY, nn	IY ← nn	●	●	●	●	●	●	11 111 101 00 100 001 ← n → ← n →	4	4	14	
LD HL, (nn)	H ← (nn+1) L ← (nn)	●	●	●	●	●	●	00 101 010 ← n → ← n →	3	5	16	
LD dd, (nn)	dd$_H$ ← (nn+1) dd$_L$ ← (nn)	●	●	●	●	●	●	11 101 101 01 dd1 011 ← n → ← n →	4	6	20	
LD IX, (nn)	IX$_H$ ← (nn+1) IX$_L$ ← (nn)	●	●	●	●	●	●	11 011 101 00 101 010 ← n → ← n →	4	6	20	
LD IY, (nn)	IY$_H$ ← (nn+1) IY$_L$ ← (nn)	●	●	●	●	●	●	11 111 101 00 101 010 ← n → ← n →	4	6	20	
LD (nn), HL	(nn+1) ← H (nn) ← L	●	●	●	●	●	●	00 100 010 ← n → ← n →	3	5	16	
LD (nn), dd	(nn+1) ← dd$_H$ (nn) ← dd$_L$	●	●	●	●	●	●	11 101 101 01 dd0 011 ← n → ← n →	4	6	20	
LD (nn), IX	(nn+1) ← IX$_H$ (nn) ← IX$_L$	●	●	●	●	●	●	11 011 101 00 100 010 ← n → ← n →	4	6	20	
LD (nn), IY	(nn+1) ← IY$_H$ (nn) ← IY$_L$	●	●	●	●	●	●	11 111 101 00 100 010 ← n → ← n →	4	6	20	
LD SP, HL	SP ← HL	●	●	●	●	●	●	11 111 001	1	1	6	
LD SP, IX	SP ← IX	●	●	●	●	●	●	11 011 101 11 111 001	2	2	10	
LD SP, IY	SP ← IY	●	●	●	●	●	●	11 111 101 11 111 001	2	2	10	qq Pair 00 BC 01 DE
PUSH qq	(SP–2) ← qq$_L$ (SP–1) ← qq$_H$	●	●	●	●	●	●	11 qq0 101	1	3	11	10 HL 11 AF
PUSH IX	(SP–2) ← IX$_L$ (SP–1) ← IX$_H$	●	●	●	●	●	●	11 011 101 11 100 101	2	4	15	
PUSH IY	(SP–2) ← IY$_L$ (SP–1) ← IY$_H$	●	●	●	●	●	●	11 111 101 11 100 101	2	4	15	
POP qq	qq$_H$ ← (SP+1) qq$_L$ ← (SP)	●	●	●	●	●	●	11 qq0 001	1	3	10	
POP IX	IX$_H$ ← (SP+1) IX$_L$ ← (SP)	●	●	●	●	●	●	11 011 101 11 100 001	2	4	14	
POP IY	IY$_H$ ← (SP+1) IY$_L$ ← (SP)	●	●	●	●	●	●	11 111 101 11 100 001	2	4	14	

Notes: dd is any of the register pairs BC, DE, HL, SP
qq is any of the register pairs AF, BC, DE, HL
(PAIR)$_H$, (PAIR)$_L$ refer to high order and low order eight bits of the register pair respectively.
E.g. BC$_L$ = C, AF$_H$ = A

Flag Notation: ● = flag not affected, 0 = flag reset, 1 = flag set, X = flag is unknown,
‡ flag is affected according to the result of the operation.

16-BIT LOAD GROUP

Mnemonic	Symbolic Operation	C	Z	P/V	S	N	H	Op-Code 76 543 210	No. of Bytes	No. of M Cycles	No. of T States	Comments
EX DE, HL	DE ·· HL	•	•	•	•	•	•	11 101 011	1	1	4	
EX AF, AF'	AF ·· AF'	•	•	•	•	•	•	00 001 000	1	1	4	
EXX	$\begin{pmatrix} BC \\ DE \\ HL \end{pmatrix} \leftrightarrow \begin{pmatrix} BC' \\ DE' \\ HL' \end{pmatrix}$	•	•	•	•	•	•	11 011 001	1	1	4	Register bank and auxiliary register bank exchange
EX (SP), HL	H ↔ (SP+1) L ↔ (SP)	•	•	•	•	•	•	11 100 011	1	5	19	
EX (SP), IX	IX$_H$ ↔ (SP+1) IX$_L$ ↔ (SP)	•	•	•	•	•	•	11 011 101 11 100 011	2	6	23	
EX (SP), IY	IY$_H$ ↔ (SP+1) IY$_L$ ↔ (SP)	•	•	•	•	•	•	11 111 101 11 100 011	2	6	23	
LDI	(DE) ← (HL) DE ← DE+1 HL ← HL+1 BC ← BC-1	•	•	① ↕	•	0	0	11 101 101 10 100 000	2	4	16	Load (HL) into (DE), increment the pointers and decrement the byte counter (BC)
LDIR	(DE) ← (HL) DE ← DE+1 HL ← HL+1 BC ← BC-1 Repeat until BC = 0	•	•	0	•	0	0	11 101 101 10 110 000	2 2	5 4	21 16	If BC ≠ 0 If BC = 0
LDD	(DE) ← (HL) DE ← DE-1 HL ← HL-1 BC ← BC-1	•	•	① ↕	•	0	0	11 101 101 10 101 000	2	4	16	
LDDR	(DE) ← (HL) DE ← DE-1 HL ← HL-1 BC ← BC-1 Repeat until BC = 0	•	•	0	•	0	0	11 101 101 10 111 000	2 2	5 4	21 16	If BC ≠ 0 If BC = 0
CPI	A – (HL) HL ← HL+1 BC ← BC- 1	•	② ↕	① ↕	↕	1	↕	11 101 101 10 100 001	2	4	16	
CPIR	A – (HL) HL ← HL+1 BC ← BC-1 Repeat until A = (HL) or BC = 0	•	② ↕	① ↕	↕	1	↕	11 101 101 10 110 001	2 2	5 4	21 16	If BC ≠ 0 and A ≠ (HL) If BC = 0 or A = (HL)
CPD	A – (HL) HL ← HL-1 BC ← BC-1	•	② ↕	① ↕	↕	1	↕	11 101 101 10 101 001	2	4	16	
CPDR	A – (HL) HL ← HL-1 BC ← BC-1 Repeat until A = (HL) or BC = 0	•	② ↕	① ↕	↕	1	↕	11 101 101 10 111 001	2 2	5 4	21 16	If BC ≠ 0 and A ≠ (HL) If BC = 0 or A = (HL)

Notes: ① P/V flag is 0 if the result of BC-1 = 0, otherwise P/V = 1

② Z flag is 1 if A = (HL), otherwise Z = 0.

Flag Notation: • = flag not affected, 0 = flag reset, 1 = flag set, X = flag is unknown,

↕ = flag is affected according to the result of the operation.

EXCHANGE GROUP AND BLOCK TRANSFER AND SEARCH GROUP

Mnemonic	Symbolic Operation	Flags						Op-Code	No. of Bytes	No. of M Cycles	No. of T States	Comments
		C	Z	P/V	S	N	H	76 543 210				
ADD A, r	A ← A + r	↕	↕	V	↕	0	↕	10 [000] r	1	1	4	r Reg.
ADD A, n	A ← A + n	↕	↕	V	↕	0	↕	11 [000] 110	2	2	7	000 B
								← n →				001 C
ADD A, (HL)	A ← A + (HL)	↕	↕	V	↕	0	↕	10 [000] 110	1	2	7	010 D
ADD A, (IX+d)	A ← A + (IX+d)	↕	↕	V	↕	0	↕	11 011 101	3	5	19	011 E
								10 [000] 110				100 H
								← d →				101 L
ADD A, (IY+d)	A ← A+(IY+d)	↕	↕	V	↕	0	↕	11 111 101	3	5	19	111 A
								10 [000] 110				
								← d →				
ADC A, s	A ← A + s + CY	↕	↕	V	↕	0	↕	[001]				s is any of r, n,
SUB s	A ← A - s	↕	↕	V	↕	1	↕	[010]				(HL), (IX+d),
SBC A, s	A ← A - s - CY	↕	↕	V	↕	1	↕	[011]				(IY+d) as shown for
AND s	A ← A ∧ s	0	↕	P	↕	0	1	[100]				ADD instruction
OR s	A ← A ∨ s	0	↕	P	↕	0	0	[110]				The indicated bits
XOR s	A ← A ⊕ s	0	↕	P	↕	0	0	[101]				replace the 000 in
CP s	A - s	↕	↕	V	↕	1	↕	[111]				the ADD set above.
INC r	r ← r + 1	•	↕	V	↕	0	↕	00 r [100]	1	1	4	
INC (HL)	(HL) ← (HL)+1	•	↕	V	↕	0	↕	00 110 [100]	1	3	11	
INC (IX+d)	(IX+d) ← (IX+d)+1	•	↕	V	↕	0	↕	11 011 101	3	6	23	
								00 110 [100]				
								← d →				
INC (IY+d)	(IY+d) ← (IY+d) + 1	•	↕	V	↕	0	↕	11 111 101	3	6	23	
								00 110 [100]				
								← d →				
DEC m	m ← m-1	•	↕	V	↕	1	↕	[101]				m is any of r, (HL), (IX+d), (IY+d) as shown for INC. Same format and states as INC. Replace 100 with 101 in OP code.

Notes: The V symbol in the P/V flag column indicates that the P/V flag contains the overflow of the result of the operation. Similarly the P symbol indicates parity. V = 1 means overflow, V = 0 means not overflow. P = 1 means parity of the result is even, P = 0 means parity of the result is odd.

Flag Notation: • = flag not affected, 0 = flag reset, 1 = flag set, X = flag is unknown.
↕ = flag is affected according to the result of the operation.

8-BIT ARITHMETIC AND LOGICAL GROUP

Mnemonic	Symbolic Operation	Flags						Op-Code	No. of Bytes	No. of M Cycles	No. of T States	Comments
		C	Z	P/V	S	N	H	76 543 210				
DAA	Converts acc. content into packed BCD following add or subtract with packed BCD operands	‡	‡	P	‡	•	‡	00 100 111	1	1	4	Decimal adjust accumulator
CPL	A ← Ā	•	•	•	•	1	1	00 101 111	1	1	4	Complement accumulator (one's complement)
NEG	A ← 0 − A	‡	‡	V	‡	1	‡	11 101 101 01 000 100	2	2	8	Negate acc. (two's complement)
CCF	CY ← $\overline{CY}$	‡	•	•	•	0	X	00 111 111	1	1	4	Complement carry flag
SCF	CY ← 1	1	•	•	•	0	0	00 110 111	1	1	4	Set carry flag
NOP	No operation	•	•	•	•	•	•	00 000 000	1	1	4	
HALT	CPU halted	•	•	•	•	•	•	01 110 110	1	1	4	
DI	IFF ← 0	•	•	•	•	•	•	11 110 011	1	1	4	
EI	IFF ← 1	•	•	•	•	•	•	11 111 011	1	1	4	
IM 0	Set interrupt mode 0	•	•	•	•	•	•	11 101 101 01 000 110	2	2	8	
IM 1	Set interrupt mode 1	•	•	•	•	•	•	11 101 101 01 010 110	2	2	8	
IM2	Set interrupt mode 2	•	•	•	•	•	•	11 101 101 01 011 110	2	2	8	

Notes: IFF indicates the interrupt enable flip-flop
CY indicates the carry flip-flop.

Flag Notation: • = flag not affected, 0 = flag reset, 1 = flag set, X = flag is unknown,
‡ = flag is affected according to the result of the operation.

GENERAL PURPOSE ARITHMETIC AND CPU CONTROL GROUPS

Mnemonic	Symbolic Operation	Flags						Op-Code	No. of Bytes	No. of M Cycles	No. of T States	Comments	
		C	Z	P/V	S	N	H	76 543 210					
ADD HL, ss	HL ← HL+ss	‡	•	•	•	0	X	00 ss1 001	1	3	11	**ss** 00 01 10 11	**Reg.** BC DE HL SP
ADC HL, ss	HL←HL+ ss +CY	‡	‡	V	‡	0	X	11 101 101 01 ss1 010	2	4	15		
SBC HL, ss	HL←HL- ss -CY	‡	‡	V	‡	1	X	11 101 101 01 ss0 010	2	4	15		
ADD IX, pp	IX ← IX + pp	‡	•	•	•	0	X	11 011 101 00 pp1 001	2	4	15	**pp** 00 01 10 11	**Reg.** BC DE IX SP
ADD IY, rr	IY←IY+ rr	‡	•	•	•	0	X	11 111 101 00 rr1 001	2	4	15	**rr** 00 01 10 11	**Reg.** BC DE IY SP
INC ss	ss ← ss + 1	•	•	•	•	•	•	00 ss0 011	1	1	6		
INC IX	IX ← IX + 1	•	•	•	•	•	•	11 011 101 00 100 011	2	2	10		
INC IY	IY ← IY + 1	•	•	•	•	•	•	11 111 101 00 100 011	2	2	10		
DEC ss	ss ← ss - 1	•	•	•	•	•	•	00 ss1 011	1	1	6		
DEC IX	IX ← IX - 1	•	•	•	•	•	•	11 011 101 00 101 011	2	2	10		
DEC IY	IY ← IY - 1	•	•	•	•	•	•	11 111 101 00 101 011	2	2	10		

Notes: ss is any of the register pairs BC, DE, HL, SP
pp is any of the register pairs BC, DE, IX, SP
rr is any of the register pairs BC, DE, IY, SP.

Flag Notation: • = flag not affected, 0 = flag reset, 1 = flag set, X = flag is unknown,
‡ = flag is affected according to the result of the operation.

16-BIT ARITHMETIC GROUP

Mnemonic	Symbolic Operation	Flags						Op-Code	No. of Bytes	No. of M Cycles	No. of T States	Comments
		C	Z	P/V	S	N	H	76 543 210				
RLCA		‡	•	•	•	0	0	00 000 111	1	1	4	Rotate left circular accumulator
RLA		‡	•	•	•	0	0	00 010 111	1	1	4	Rotate left accumulator
RRCA		‡	•	•	•	0	0	00 001 111	1	1	4	Rotate right circular accumulator
RRA		‡	•	•	•	0	0	00 011 111	1	1	4	Rotate right accumulator
RLC r		‡	‡	P	‡	0	0	11 001 011 00 000 r	2	2	8	Rotate left circular register r
RLC (HL)		‡	‡	P	‡	0	0	11 001 011 00 000 110	2	4	15	
RLC (IX+d)		‡	‡	P	‡	0	0	11 011 101 11 001 011 ← d → 00 000 '10	4	6	23	
RLC (IY+d)		‡	‡	P	‡	0	0	11 111 101 11 001 011 ← d → 00 000 110	4	6	23	

r	Reg.
000	B
001	C
010	D
011	E
100	H
101	L
111	A

Mnemonic	Symbolic Operation	Flags						Op-Code	No. of Bytes	No. of M Cycles	No. of T States	Comments
RL m	 m ≡ r, (HL), (IX+d), (IY+d)	‡	‡	P	‡	0	0	010				Instruction format and states are as shown for RLC,m. To form new OP-code replace 000 of RLC,m with shown code
RRC m	 m ≡ r, (HL), (IX+d), (IY+d)	‡	‡	P	‡	0	0	001				
RR m	 m ≡ r, (HL), (IX+d), (IY+d)	‡	‡	P	‡	0	0	011				
SLA m	 m ≡ r, (HL), (IX+d), (IY+d)	‡	‡	P	‡	0	0	100				
SRA m	 m ≡ r, (HL), (IX+d), (IY+d)	‡	‡	P	‡	0	0	101				
SRL m	 m ≡ r, (HL), (IX+d), (IY+d)	‡	‡	P	‡	0	0	111				
RLD		•	‡	P	‡	0	0	11 101 101 01 101 111	2	5	18	Rotate digit left and right between the accumulator and location (HL). The content of the upper half of the accumulator is unaffected
RRD		•	‡	P	‡	0	0	11 101 101 01 100 111	2	5	18	

Flag Notation: • = flag not affected, 0 = flag reset, 1 = flag set, X = flag is unknown,
‡ = flag is affected according to the result of the operation.

ROTATE AND SHIFT GROUP

Mnemonic	Symbolic Operation	Flags C	Z	P/V	S	N	H	Op-Code 76 543 210	No. of Bytes	No. of M Cycles	No. of T States	Comments
BIT b, r	$Z \leftarrow \overline{r_b}$	•	‡	X	X	0	1	11 001 011 01 b r	2	2	8	
BIT b, (HL)	$Z \leftarrow \overline{(HL)_b}$	•	‡	X	X	0	1	11 001 011 01 b 110	2	3	12	
BIT b, (IX+d)	$Z \leftarrow \overline{(IX+d)_b}$	•	‡	X	X	0	1	11 011 101 11 001 011 ← d → 01 b 110	4	5	20	
BIT b, (IY+d)	$Z \leftarrow \overline{(IY+d)_b}$	•	‡	X	X	0	1	11 111 101 11 001 011 ← d → 01 b 110	4	5	20	
SET b, r	$r_b \leftarrow 1$	•	•	•	•	•	•	11 001 011 [11] b r	2	2	8	
SET b, (HL)	$(HL)_b \leftarrow 1$	•	•	•	•	•	•	11 001 011 [11] b 110	2	4	15	
SET b, (IX+d)	$(IX+d)_b \leftarrow 1$	•	•	•	•	•	•	11 011 101 11 001 011 ← d → [11] b 110	4	6	23	
SET b, (IY+d)	$(IY+d)_b \leftarrow 1$	•	•	•	•	•	•	11 111 101 11 001 011 ← d → [11] b 110	4	6	23	
RES b, m	$s_b \leftarrow 0$ $m \equiv r, (HL),$ $(IX+d),$ $(IY+d)$							[10]				To form new OP-code replace [11] of SET b,m with [10]. Flags and time states for SET instruction

Comments (register/bit tables):

r	Reg.
000	B
001	C
010	D
011	E
100	H
101	L
111	A

b	Bit Tested
000	0
001	1
010	2
011	3
100	4
101	5
110	6
111	7

Notes: The notation s_b indicates bit b (0 to 7) or location s.

Flag Notation: • = flag not affected, 0 = flag reset, 1 = flag set, X = flag is unknown,
‡ = flag is affected according to the result of the operation.

BIT SET, RESET AND TEST GROUP

Mnemonic	Symbolic Operation	Flags						Op-Code	No. of Bytes	No. of M Cycles	No. of T States	Comments
		C	Z	P/V	S	N	H	76 543 210				
JP nn	PC ← nn	•	•	•	•	•	•	11 000 011	3	3	10	
								← n →				
								← n →				
JP cc, nn	If condition cc is true PC ←nn, otherwise continue	•	•	•	•	•	•	11 cc 010	3	3	10	
								← n →				
								← n →				
JR e	PC ← PC + e	•	•	•	•	•	•	00 011 000	2	3	12	
								← e-2 →				
JR C, e	If C = 0, continue	•	•	•	•	•	•	00 111 000	2	2	7	If condition not met
								← e-2 →				
	If C = 1, PC ← PC+e								2	3	12	If condition is met
JR NC, e	If C = 1, continue	•	•	•	•	•	•	00 110 000	2	2	7	If condition not met
								← e-2 →				
	If C = 0, PC ← PC + e								2	3	12	If condition is met
JR Z, e	If Z = 0 continue	•	•	•	•	•	•	00 101 000	2	2	7	If condition not met
								← e-2 →				
	If Z = 1, PC ← PC + e								2	3	12	If condition is met
JR NZ, e	If Z = 1, continue	•	•	•	•	•	•	00 100 000	2	2	7	If condition not met
								← e-2 →				
	If Z = 0, PC ← PC + e								2	3	12	If condition met
JP (HL)	PC ← HL	•	•	•	•	•	•	11 101 001	1	1	4	
JP (IX)	PC ← IX	•	•	•	•	•	•	11 011 101	2	2	8	
								11 101 001				
JP (IY)	PC ← IY	•	•	•	•	•	•	11 111 101	2	2	8	
								11 101 001				
DJNZ,e	B ← B-1 If B = 0, continue	•	•	•	•	•	•	00 010 000	2	2	8	If B = 0
								← e-2 →				
	If B ≠ 0, PC ← PC + e								2	3	13	IF B ≠ 0

cc	Condition
000	NZ non zero
001	Z zero
010	NC non carry
011	C carry
100	PO parity odd
101	PE parity even
110	P sign positive
111	M sign negative

Notes: e represents the extension in the relative addressing mode.

e is a signed two's complement number in the range $<-126, 129>$

e-2 in the op-code provides an effective address of pc +e as PC is incremented by 2 prior to the addition of e.

Flag Notation: • = flag not affected, 0 = flag reset, 1 = flag set, X = flag is unknown,

‡ = flag is affected according to the result of the operation.

JUMP GROUP

Mnemonic	Symbolic Operation	Flags						Op-Code	No. of Bytes	No. of M Cycles	No. of T States	Comments
		C	Z	P/V	S	N	H	76 543 210				
CALL nn	$(SP-1) \leftarrow PC_H$ $(SP-2) \leftarrow PC_L$ $PC \leftarrow nn$	•	•	•	•	•	•	11 001 101 ← n → ← n →	3	5	17	
CALL cc, nn	If condition cc is false continue, otherwise same as CALL nn	•	•	•	•	•	•	11 cc 100 ← n → ← n →	3 3	3 5	10 17	If cc is false If cc is true
RET	$PC_L \leftarrow (SP)$ $PC_H \leftarrow (SP+1)$	•	•	•	•	•	•	11 001 001	1	3	10	
RET cc	If condition cc is false continue, otherwise same as RET	•	•	•	•	•	•	11 cc 000	1 1	1 3	5 11	If cc is false If cc is true
RETI	Return from interrupt	•	•	•	•	•	•	11 101 101 01 001 101	2	4	14	
RETN	Return from non maskable interrupt	•	•	•	•	•	•	11 101 101 01 000 101	2	4	14	
RST p	$(SP-1) \leftarrow PC_H$ $(SP-2) \leftarrow PC_L$ $PC_H \leftarrow 0$ $PC_L \leftarrow P$	•	•	•	•	•	•	11 t 111	1	3	11	

cc		Condition
000	NZ	non zero
001	Z	zero
010	NC	non carry
011	C	carry
100	PO	parity odd
101	PE	parity even
110	P	sign positive
111	M	sign negative

t	P
000	00H
001	08H
010	10H
011	18H
100	20H
101	28H
110	30H
111	38H

Flag Notation: • = flag not affected, 0 = flag reset, 1 = flag set, X = flag is unknown
‡ = flag is affected according to the result of the operation.

CALL AND RETURN GROUP

Mnemonic	Symbolic Operation	Flags						Op-Code	No. of Bytes	No. of M Cycles	No. of T States	Comments
		C	Z	P/V	S	N	H	76 543 210				
IN A, (n)	A ← (n)	•	•	•	•	•	•	11 011 011	2	3	11	n to A_0 ~ A_7
								← n →				Acc to A_8 ~ A_{15}
IN r, (C)	r ← (C)	•	‡	P	‡	0	‡	11 101 101	2	3	12	C to A_0 ~ A_7
	if r = 110 only the flags will be affected							01 r 000				B to A_8 ~ A_{15}
INI	(HL) ← (C)	X	‡ ①	X	X	1	X	11 101 101	2	4	16	C to A_0 ~ A_7
	B ← B - 1							10 100 010				B to A_8 ~ A_{15}
	HL ← HL + 1											
INIR	(HL) ← (C)	X	1	X	X	1	X	11 101 101	2	5 (If B ≠ 0)	21	C to A_0 ~ A_7
	B ← B - 1							10 110 010				B to A_8 ~ A_{15}
	HL ← HL + 1								2	4 (If B = 0)	16	
	Repeat until B = 0											
IND	(HL) ← (C)	X	‡ ①	X	X	1	X	11 101 101	2	4	16	C to A_0 ~ A_7
	B ← B - 1							10 101 010				B to A_8 ~ A_{15}
	HL ← HL - 1											
INDR	(HL) ← (C)	X	1	X	X	1	X	11 101 101	2	5 (If B ≠ 0)	21	C to A_0 ~ A_7
	B ← B - 1							10 111 010				B to A_8 ~ A_{15}
	HL ← HL -1								2	4 (If B = 0)	16	
	Repeat until B = 0											
OUT (n), A	(n) ← A	•	•	•	•	•	•	11 010 011	2	3	11	n to A_0 ~ A_7
								← n →				Acc to A_8 ~ A_{15}
OUT (C), r	(C) ← r	•	•	•	•	•	•	11 101 101	2	3	12	C to A_0 ~ A_7
								01 r 001				B to A_8 ~ A_{15}
OUTI	(C) ← (HL)	X	‡ ①	X	X	1	X	11 101 101	2	4	16	C to A_0 ~ A_7
	B ← B - 1							10 100 011				B to A_8 ~ A_{15}
	HL ← HL + 1											
OTIR	(C) ← (HL)	X	1	X	X	1	X	11 101 101	2	5 (If B ≠ 0)	21	C to A_0 ~ A_7
	B ← B - 1							10 110 011				B to A_8 ~ A_{15}
	HL ← HL + 1								2	4 (If B = 0)	16	
	Repeat until B = 0											
OUTD	(C) ← (HL)	X	‡ ①	X	X	1	X	11 101 101	2	4	16	C to A_0 ~ A_7
	B ← B - 1							10 101 011				B to A_8 ~ A_{15}
	HL ← HL - 1											
OTDR	(C) ← (HL)	X	1	X	X	1	X	11 101 101	2	5 (If B ≠ 0)	21	C to A_0 ~ A_7
	B ← B - 1							10 111 011				B to A_8 ~ A_{15}
	HL ← HL -1								2	4 (If B = 0)	16	
	Repeat until B = 0											

Notes: ① If the result of B - 1 is zero the Z flag is set, otherwise it is reset .

Flag Notation: • = flag not affected, 0 = flag reset, 1 = flag set, X = flag is unknown,
‡ = flag is affected according to the result of the operation.

INPUT AND OUTPUT GROUP

APPENDIX B: ASCII/Hexadecimal Conversion Table

LSD	MSD	Ø ØØØ	1 ØØ1	2 Ø1Ø	3 Ø11	4 1ØØ	5 1Ø1	6 11Ø	7 111
Ø	ØØØØ	NUL	DLE	SPACE	Ø	@	P	@	p
1	ØØØ1	SOH	DC1	!	1	A	Q	a	q
2	ØØ1Ø	STX	DC2	"	2	B	R	b	r
3	ØØ11	ETX	DC3	#	3	C	S	c	s
4	Ø1ØØ	EOT	DC4	$	4	D	T	d	t
5	Ø1Ø1	ENQ	NAK	%	5	E	U	e	u
6	Ø11Ø	ACK	SYN	&	6	F	V	f	v
7	Ø111	BEL	ETB	'	7	G	W	g	w
8	1ØØØ	BS	CAN	(	8	H	X	h	X
9	1ØØ1	HT	EM	)	9	I	Y	i	y
A	1Ø1Ø	LF	SUB	*	:	J	Z	j	z
B	1Ø11	VT	ESC	+	;	K	up ar	k	up ar
C	11ØØ	FF	FS	,	<	L	dn ar	l	dn ar
D	11Ø1	CR	GS	-	=	M	lf ar	m	lf ar
E	111Ø	SO	RS	.	>	N	rt ar	n	rt ar
F	1111	SI	US	/	?	O	cursor	o	DEL

This table shows the correspondence between ASCII characters
and their hexadecimal values. To read the chart, take the
most-significant digit from the top row and the least-
significant digit from the left column.

The following abbreviations have been used to indicate special
functions:

NUL		NULL	DLE	Data Link Escape
SOH	*	Start of Heading	DC1	Device Control 1
STX		Start of Text	DC2	Device Control 2
ETX		End of Text	DC3	Device Control 3
EOT		End of Transmission	DC4	Device Control 4
ENQ		Enquiry	NAK	Negative Acknowledge
ACK		Acknowledge	SYN	Synchronous Idle
BEL		Bell	ETB	* End of Transmission
DEL		Delete		Block
BS		Backspace	CAN	Cancel
HT		Horizontal Tabulation	EM	End of Medium
LF		Line Feed	SS	Special Sequence
VT		Vertical Tabulation	ESC	Escape
FF		Form Feed	FS	* File Separator
CR		Carriage Return	GS	* Group Separator
SO	*	Shift Out	RS	* Record Separator
SI	*	Shift In	US	* Unit Separator

The special functions marked with an asterisk have been given
special meanings on the TRS-80, and hence the normal ASCII
function is not available.   These special meanings are as
follows:

Char	Value	Meaning
SOH	Ø1	BREAK key
SO	ØE	Cursor On
SI	ØF	Cursor Off
ETB	17	32-character mode
FS	1C	Home Cursor
GS	1D	Cursor to beginning of line
RS	1E	Erase to end of line
US	1F	Clear to end of screen

In addition to these changes, it is also necessary to note
that Radio Shack did not use standard ASCII values for the
down arrow, left arrow, right arrow, cursor, and "shift-@"
keys.

APPENDIX C: Numeric List of Z-80 Instructions

OBJECT CODE	SOURCE STATEMENT		OBJECT CODE	SOURCE STATEMENT	
00	NOP		328405	LD	(NN),A
018405	LD	BC,NN	33	INC	SP
02	LD	(BC),A	34	INC	(HL)
03	INC	BC	35	DEC	(HL)
04	INC	B	3620	LD	(HL),N
05	DEC	B	37	SCF	
0620	LD	B,N	382E	JR	C,DIS
07	RLCA		39	ADD	HL,SP
08	EX	AF,AF'	3A8405	LD	A,(NN)
09	ADD	HL,BC	3B	DEC	SP
0A	LD	A,(BC)	3C	INC	A
0B	DEC	BC	3D	DEC	A
0C	INC	C	3E20	LD	A,N
0D	DEC	C	3F	CCF	
0E20	LD	C,N	40	LD	B,B
0F	RRCA		41	LD	B,C
102E	DJNZ	DIS	42	LD	B,D
118405	LD	DE,NN	43	LD	B,E
12	LD	(DE),A	44	LD	B,H
13	INC	DE	45	LD	B,L
14	INC	D	46	LD	B,(HL)
15	DEC	D	47	LD	B,A
1620	LD	D,N	48	LD	C,B
17	RLA		49	LD	C,C
182E	JR	DIS	4A	LD	C,D
19	ADD	HL,DE	4B	LD	C,E
1A	LD	A,(DE)	4C	LD	C,H
1B	DEC	DE	4D	LD	C,L
1C	INC	E	4E	LD	C,(HL)
1D	DEC	E	4F	LD	C,A
1E20	LD	E,N	50	LD	D,B
1F	RRA		51	LD	D,C
202E	JR	NZ,DIS	52	LD	D,D
218405	LD	HL,NN	53	LD	D,E
228405	LD	(NN),HL	54	LD	D,H
23	INC	HL	55	LD	D,L
24	INC	H	56	LD	D,(HL)
25	DEC	H	57	LD	D,A
2620	LD	H,N	58	LD	E,B
27	DAA		59	LD	E,C
282E	JR	Z,DIS	5A	LD	E,D
29	ADD	HL,HL	5B	LD	E,E
2A8405	LD	HL,(NN)	5C	LD	E,H
2B	DEC	HL	5D	LD	E,L
2C	INC	L	5E	LD	E,(HL)
2D	DEC	L	5F	LD	E,A
2E20	LD	L,N	60	LD	H,B
2F	CPL		61	LD	H,C
302E	JR	NC,DIS	62	LD	H,D
318405	LD	SP,NN	63	LD	H,E

OBJECT CODE	SOURCE STATEMENT		OBJECT CODE	SOURCE STATEMENT	
64	LD	H,H	96	SUB	(HL)
65	LD	H,L	97	SUB	A
66	LD	H,(HL)	98	SBC	A,B
67	LD	H,A	99	SBC	A,C
68	LD	L,B	9A	SBC	A,D
69	LD	L,C	9B	SBC	A,E
6A	LD	L,D	9C	SBC	A,H
6B	LD	L,E	9D	SBC	A,L
6C	LD	L,H	9E	SBC	A,(HL)
6D	LD	L,L	9F	SBC	A,A
6E	LD	L,(HL)	A0	AND	B
6F	LD	L,A	A1	AND	C
70	LD	(HL),B	A2	AND	D
71	LD	(HL),C	A3	AND	E
72	LD	(HL),D	A4	AND	H
73	LD	(HL),E	A5	AND	L
74	LD	(HL),H	A6	AND	(HL)
75	LD	(HL),L	A7	AND	A
76	HALT		A8	XOR	B
77	LD	(HL),A	A9	XOR	C
78	LD	A,B	AA	XOR	D
79	LD	A,C	AB	XOR	E
7A	LD	A,D	AC	XOR	H
7B	LD	A,E	AD	XOR	L
7C	LD	A,H	AE	XOR	(HL)
7D	LD	A,L	AF	XOR	A
7E	LD	A,(HL)	B0	OR	B
7F	LD	A,A	B1	OR	C
80	ADD	A,B	B2	OR	D
81	ADD	A,C	B3	OR	E
82	ADD	A,D	B4	OR	H
83	ADD	A,E	B5	OR	L
84	ADD	A,H	B6	OR	(HL)
85	ADD	A,L	B7	OR	A
86	ADD	A,(HL)	B8	CP	B
87	ADD	A,A	B9	CP	C
88	ADC	A,B	BA	CP	D
89	ADC	A,C	BB	CP	E
8A	ADC	A,D	BC	CP	H
8B	ADC	A,E	BD	CP	L
8C	ADC	A,H	BE	CP	(HL)
8D	ADC	A,L	BF	CP	A
8E	ADC	A,(HL)	C0	RET	NZ
8F	ADC	A,A	C1	POP	BC
90	SUB	B	C28405	JP	NZ,NN
91	SUB	C	C38405	JP	NN
92	SUB	D	C48405	CALL	NZ,NN
93	SUB	E	C5	PUSH	BC
94	SUB	H	C620	ADD	A,N
95	SUB	L	C7	RST	0

OBJECT CODE	SOURCE STATEMENT		OBJECT CODE	SOURCE STATEMENT	
C8	RET	Z	FA8405	JP	M,NN
C9	RET		FB	EI	
CA8405	JP	Z,NN	FC8405	CALL	M,NN
CBnn	see below		FDnnnnnn	see below	
CC8405	CALL	Z,NN	FE20	CP	N
CD8405	CALL	NN	FF	RST	38H
CE20	ADC	A,N	CB00	RLC	B
CF	RST	8	CB01	RLC	C
D0	RET	NC	CB02	RLC	D
D1	POP	DE	CB03	RLC	E
D28405	JP	NC,NN	CB04	RLC	H
D320	OUT	(N),A	CB05	RLC	L
D48405	CALL	NC,NN	CB06	RLC	(HL)
D5	PUSH	DE	CB07	RLC	A
D620	SUB	N	CB08	RRC	B
D7	RST	10H	CB09	RRC	C
D8	RET	C	CB0A	RRC	D
D9	EXX		CB0B	RRC	E
DA8405	JP	C,NN	CB0C	RRC	H
DB20	IN	A,(N)	CB0D	RRC	L
DC8405	CALL	C,NN	CB0E	RRC	(HL)
DDnnnnnn	see below		CB0F	RRC	A
DE20	SBC	A,N	CB10	RL	B
DF	RST	18H	CB11	RL	C
E0	RET	PO	CB12	RL	D
E1	POP	HL	CB13	RL	E
E28405	JP	PO,NN	CB14	RL	H
E3	EX	(SP),HL	CB15	RL	L
E48405	CALL	PO,NN	CB16	RL	(HL)
E5	PUSH	HL	CB17	RL	A
E620	AND	N	CB18	RR	B
E7	RST	20H	CB19	RR	C
E8	RET	PE	CB1A	RR	D
E9	JP	(HL)	CB1B	RR	E
EA8405	JP	PE,NN	CB1C	RR	H
EB	EX	DE,HL	CB1D	RR	L
EC8405	CALL	PE,NN	CB1E	RR	(HL)
EDnnnnnn	see below		CB1F	RR	A
EE20	XOR	N	CB20	SLA	B
EF	RST	28H	CB21	SLA	C
F0	RET	P	CB22	SLA	D
F1	POP	AF	CB23	SLA	E
F28405	JP	P,NN	CB24	SLA	H
F3	DI		CB25	SLA	L
F48405	CALL	P,NN	CB26	SLA	(HL)
F5	PUSH	AF	CB27	SLA	A
F620	OR	N	CB28	SRA	B
F7	RST	30H	CB29	SRA	C
F8	RET	M	CB2A	SRA	D
F9	LD	SP,HL	CB2B	SRA	E

OBJECT CODE	SOURCE STATEMENT		OBJECT CODE	SOURCE STATEMENT	
CB2C	SRA	H	CB66	BIT	4,(HL)
CB2D	SRA	L	CB67	BIT	4,A
CB2E	SRA	(HL)	CB68	BIT	5,B
CB2F	SRA	A	CB69	BIT	5,C
CB38	SRL	B	CB6A	BIT	5,D
CB39	SRL	C	CB6B	BIT	5,E
CB3A	SRL	D	CB6C	BIT	5,H
CB3B	SRL	E	CB6D	BIT	5,L
CB3C	SRL	H	CB6E	BIT	5,(HL)
CB3D	SRL	L	CB6F	BIT	5,A
CB3E	SRL	(HL)	CB70	BIT	6,B
CB3F	SRL	A	CB71	BIT	6,C
CB40	BIT	0,B	CB72	BIT	6,D
CB41	BIT	0,C	CB73	BIT	6,E
CB42	BIT	0,D	CB74	BIT	6,H
CB43	BIT	0,E	CB75	BIT	6,L
CB44	BIT	0,H	CB76	BIT	6,(HL)
CB45	BIT	0,L	CB77	BIT	6,A
CB46	BIT	0,(HL)	CB78	BIT	7,B
CB47	BIT	0,A	CB79	BIT	7,C
CB48	BIT	1,B	CB7A	BIT	7,D
CB49	BIT	1,C	CB7B	BIT	7,E
CB4A	BIT	1,D	CB7C	BIT	7,H
CB4B	BIT	1,E	CB7D	BIT	7,L
CB4C	BIT	1,H	CB7E	BIT	7,(HL)
CB4D	BIT	1,L	CB7F	BIT	7,A
CB4E	BIT	1,(HL)	CB80	RES	0,B
CB4F	BIT	1,A	CB81	RES	0,C
CB50	BIT	2,B	CB82	RES	0,D
CB51	BIT	2,C	CB83	RES	0,E
CB52	BIT	2,D	CB84	RES	0,H
CB53	BIT	2,E	CB85	RES	0,L
CB54	BIT	2,H	CB86	RES	0,(HL)
CB55	BIT	2,L	CB87	RES	0,A
CB56	BIT	2,(HL)	CB88	RES	1,B
CB57	BIT	2,A	CB89	RES	1,C
CB58	BIT	3,B	CB8A	RES	1,D
CB59	BIT	3,C	CB8B	RES	1,E
CB5A	BIT	3,D	CB8C	RES	1,H
CB5B	BIT	3,E	CB8D	RES	1,L
CB5C	BIT	3,H	CB8E	RES	1,(HL)
CB5D	BIT	3,L	CB8F	RES	1,A
CB5E	BIT	3,(HL)	CB90	RES	2,B
CB5F	BIT	3,A	CB91	RES	2,C
CB60	BIT	4,B	CB92	RES	2,D
CB61	BIT	4,C	CB93	RES	2,E
CB62	BIT	4,D	CB94	RES	2,H
CB63	BIT	4,E	CB95	RES	2,L
CB64	BIT	4,H	CB96	RES	2,(HL)
CB65	BIT	4,L	CB97	RES	2,A

OBJECT CODE	SOURCE STATEMENT		OBJECT CODE	SOURCE STATEMENT	
CB98	RES	3,B	CBCA	SET	1,D
CB99	RES	3,C	CBCB	SET	1,E
CB9A	RES	3,D	CBCC	SET	1,H
CB9B	RES	3,E	CBCD	SET	1,L
CB9C	RES	3,H	CBCE	SET	1,(HL)
CB9D	RES	3,L	CBCF	SET	1,A
CB9E	RES	3,(HL)	CBD0	SET	2,B
CB9F	RES	3,A	CBD1	SET	2,C
CBA0	RES	4,B	CBD2	SET	2,D
CBA1	RES	4,C	CBD3	SET	2,E
CBA2	RES	4,D	CBD4	SET	2,H
CBA3	RES	4,E	CBD5	SET	2,L
CBA4	RES	4,H	CBD6	SET	2,(HL)
CBA5	RES	4,L	CBD7	SET	2,A
CBA6	RES	4,(HL)	CBD8	SET	3,B
CBA7	RES	4,A	CBD9	SET	3,C
CBA8	RES	5,B	CBDA	SET	3,D
CBA9	RES	5,C	CBDB	SET	3,E
CBAA	RES	5,D	CBDC	SET	3,H
CBAB	RES	5,E	CBDD	SET	3,L
CBAC	RES	5,H	CBDE	SET	3,(HL)
CBAD	RES	5,L	CBDF	SET	3,A
CBAE	RES	5,(HL)	CBE0	SET	4,B
CBAF	RES	5,A	CBE1	SET	4,C
CBB0	RES	6,B	CBE2	SET	4,D
CBB1	RES	6,C	CBE3	SET	4,E
CBB2	RES	6,D	CBE4	SET	4,H
CBB3	RES	6,E	CBE5	SET	4,L
CBB4	RES	6,H	CBE6	SET	4,(HL)
CBB5	RES	6,L	CBE7	SET	4,A
CBB6	RES	6,(HL)	CBE8	SET	5,B
CBB7	RES	6,A	CBE9	SET	5,C
CBB8	RES	7,B	CBEA	SET	5,D
CBB9	RES	7,C	CBEB	SET	5,E
CBBA	RES	7,D	CBEC	SET	5,H
CBBB	RES	7,E	CBED	SET	5,L
CBBC	RES	7,H	CBEE	SET	5,(HL)
CBBD	RES	7,L	CBEF	SET	5,A
CBBE	RES	7,(HL)	CBF0	SET	6,B
CBBF	RES	7,A	CBF1	SET	6,C
CBC0	SET	0,B	CBF2	SET	6,D
CBC1	SET	0,C	CBF3	SET	6,E
CBC2	SET	0,D	CBF4	SET	6,H
CBC3	SET	0,E	CBF5	SET	6,L
CBC4	SET	0,H	CBF6	SET	6,(HL)
CBC5	SET	0,L	CBF7	SET	6,A
CBC6	SET	0,(HL)	CBF8	SET	7,B
CBC7	SET	0,A	CBF9	SET	7,C
CBC8	SET	1,B	CBFA	SET	7,D
CBC9	SET	1,C	CBFB	SET	7,E

OBJECT CODE	SOURCE STATEMENT		OBJECT CODE	SOURCE STATEMENT	
CBFC	SET	7,H	DDCB0546	BIT	0,(IX+IND)
CBFD	SET	7,L	DDCB054E	BIT	1,(IX+IND)
CBFE	SET	7,(HL)	DDCB0556	BIT	2,(IX+IND)
CBFF	SET	7,A	DDCB055E	BIT	3,(IX+IND)
DD09	ADD	IX,BC	DDCB0566	BIT	4,(IX+IND)
DD19	ADD	IX,DE	DDCB056E	BIT	5,(IX+IND)
DD218405	LD	IX,NN	DDCB0576	BIT	6,(IX+IND)
DD228405	LD	(NN),IX	DDCB057E	BIT	7,(IX+IND)
DD23	INC	IX	DDCB0586	RES	0,(IX+IND)
DD29	ADD	IX,IX	DDCB058E	RES	1,(IX+IND)
DD2A8405	LD	IX,(NN)	DDCB0596	RES	2,(IX+IND)
DD2B	DEC	IX	DDCB059E	RES	3,(IX+IND)
DD3405	INC	(IX+IND)	DDCB05A6	RES	4,(IX+IND)
DD3505	DEC	(IX+IND)	DDCB05AE	RES	5,(IX+IND)
DD360520	LD	(IX+IND),N	DDCB05B6	RES	6,(IX+IND)
DD39	ADD	IX,SP	DDCB05BE	RES	7,(IX+IND)
DD4605	LD	B,(IX+IND)	DDCB05C6	SET	0,(IX+IND)
DD4E05	LD	C,(IX+IND)	DDCB05CE	SET	1,(IX+IND)
DD5605	LD	D,(IX+IND)	DDCB05D6	SET	2,(IX+IND)
DD5E05	LD	E,(IX+IND)	DDCB05DE	SET	3,(IX+IND)
DD6605	LD	H,(IX+IND)	DDCB05E6	SET	4,(IX+IND)
DD6E05	LD	L,(IX+IND)	DDCB05EE	SET	5,(IX+IND)
DD7005	LD	(IX+IND),B	DDCB05F6	SET	6,(IX+IND)
DD7105	LD	(IX+IND),C	DDCB05FE	SET	7,(IX+IND)
DD7205	LD	(IX+IND),D	ED40	IN	B,(C)
DD7305	LD	(IX+IND),E	ED41	OUT	(C),B
DD7405	LD	(IX+IND),H	ED42	SBC	HL,BC
DD7505	LD	(IX+IND),L	ED438405	LD	(NN),BC
DD7705	LD	(IX+IND),A	ED44	NEG	
DD7E05	LD	A,(IX+IND)	ED45	RETN	
DD8605	ADD	A,(IX+IND)	ED46	IM	0
DD8E05	ADC	A,(IX+IND)	ED47	LD	I,A
DD9605	SUB	(IX+IND)	ED48	IN	C,(C)
DD9E05	SBC	A,(IX+IND)	ED49	OUT	(C),C
DDA605	AND	(IX+IND)	ED4A	ADC	HL,BC
DDAE05	XOR	(IX+IND)	ED4B8405	LD	BC,(NN)
DDB605	OR	(IX+IND)	ED4D	RETI	
DDBE05	CP	(IX+IND)	ED4F	LD	R,A
DDE1	POP	IX	ED50	IN	D,(C)
DDE3	EX	(SP),IX	ED51	OUT	(C),D
DDE5	PUSH	IX	ED52	SBC	HL,DE
DDE9	JP	(IX)	ED538405	LD	(NN),DE
DDF9	LD	SP,IX	ED56	IM	1
DDCB0506	RLC	(IX+IND)	ED57	LD	A,I
DDCB050E	RRC	(IX+IND)	ED58	IN	E,(C)
DDCB0516	RL	(IX+IND)	ED59	OUT	(C),E
DDCB051E	RR	(IX+IND)	ED5A	ADC	HL,DE
DDCB0526	SLA	(IX+IND)	ED5B8405	LD	DE,(NN)
DDCB052E	SRA	(IX+IND)	ED5E	IM	2
DDCB053E	SRL	(IX+IND)	ED5F	LD	A,R

OBJECT CODE	SOURCE STATEMENT		OBJECT CODE	SOURCE STATEMENT	
ED60	IN	H,(C)	FD7305	LD	(IY+IND),E
ED61	OUT	(C),H	FD7405	LD	(IY+IND),H
ED62	SBC	HL,HL	FD7505	LD	(IY+IND),L
ED67	RRD		FD7705	LD	(IY+IND),A
ED68	IN	L,(C)	FD7E05	LD	A,(IY+IND)
ED69	OUT	(C),L	FD8605	ADD	A,(IY+IND)
ED6A	ADC	HL,HL	FD8E05	ADC	A,(IY+IND)
ED6F	RLD		FD9605	SUB	(IY+IND)
ED72	SBC	HL,SP	FD9E05	SBC	A,(IY+IND)
ED738405	LD	(NN),SP	FDA605	AND	(IY+IND)
ED78	IN	A,(C)	FDAE05	XOR	(IY+IND)
ED79	OUT	(C),A	FDB605	OR	(IY+IND)
ED7A	ADC	HL,SP	FDBE05	CP	(IY+IND)
ED7B8405	LD	SP,(NN)	FDE1	POP	IY
EDA0	LDI		FDE3	EX	(SP),IY
EDA1	CPI		FDE5	PUSH	IY
EDA2	INI		FDE9	JP	(IY)
EDA3	OUTI		FDF9	LD	SP,IY
EDA8	LDD		FDCB0506	RLC	(IY+IND)
EDA9	CPD		FDCB050E	RRC	(IY+IND)
EDAA	IND		FDCB0516	RL	(IY+IND)
EDAB	OUTD		FDCB051E	RR	(IY+IND)
EDB0	LDIR		FDCB0526	SLA	(IY+IND)
EDB1	CPIR		FDCB052E	SRA	(IY+IND)
EDB2	INIR		FDCB053E	SRL	(IY+IND)
EDB3	OTIR		FDCB0546	BIT	0,(IY+IND)
EDB8	LDDR		FDCB054E	BIT	1,(IY+IND)
EDB9	CPDR		FDCB0556	BIT	2,(IY+IND)
EDBA	INDR		FDCB055E	BIT	3,(IY+IND)
EDBB	OTDR		FDCB0566	BIT	4,(IY+IND)
FD09	ADD	IY,BC	FDCB056E	BIT	5,(IY+IND)
FD19	ADD	IY,DE	FDCB0576	BIT	6,(IY+IND)
FD218405	LD	IY,NN	FDCB057E	BIT	7,(IY+IND)
FD228405	LD	(NN),IY	FDCB0586	RES	0,(IY+IND)
FD23	INC	IY	FDCB058E	RES	1,(IY+IND)
FD29	ADD	IY,IY	FDCB0596	RES	2,(IY+IND)
FD2A8405	LD	IY,(NN)	FDCB059E	RES	3,(IY+IND)
FD2B	DEC	IY	FDCB05A6	RES	4,(IY+IND)
FD3405	INC	(IY+IND)	FDCB05AE	RES	5,(IY+IND)
FD3505	DEC	(IY+IND)	FDCB05B6	RES	6,(IY+IND)
FD360520	LD	(IY+IND),N	FDCB05BE	RES	7,(IY+IND)
FD39	ADD	IY,SP	FDCB05C6	SET	0,(IY+IND)
FD4605	LD	B,(IY+IND)	FDCB05CE	SET	1,(IY+IND)
FD4E05	LD	C,(IY+IND)	FDCB05D6	SET	2,(IY+IND)
FD5605	LD	D,(IY+IND)	FDCB05DE	SET	3,(IY+IND)
FD5E05	LD	E,(IY+IND)	FDCB05E6	SET	4,(IY+IND)
FD6605	LD	H,(IY+IND)	FDCB05EE	SET	5,(IY+IND)
FD6E05	LD	L,(IY+IND)	FDCB05F6	SET	6,(IY+IND)
FD7005	LD	(IY+IND),B	FDCB05FE	SET	7,(IY+IND)
FD7105	LD	(IY+IND),C			
FD7205	LD	(IY+IND),D			

APPENDIX D: Alphabetic List of Z-80 Instructions

OBJECT CODE	SOURCE STATEMENT		OBJECT CODE	SOURCE STATEMENT	
8E	ADC	A,(HL)	DDCB0546	BIT	0,(IX+IND)
DD8E05	ADC	A,(IX+IND)	FDCB0546	BIT	0,(IY+IND)
FD8E05	ADC	A,(IY+IND)	CB47	BIT	0,A
8F	ADC	A,A	CB40	BIT	0,B
88	ADC	A,B	CB41	BIT	0,C
89	ADC	A,C	CB42	BIT	0,D
8A	ADC	A,D	CB43	BIT	0,E
8B	ADC	A,E	CB44	BIT	0,H
8C	ADC	A,H	CB45	BIT	0,L
8D	ADC	A,L	CB4E	BIT	1,(HL)
CE20	ADC	A,N	DDCB054E	BIT	1,(IX+IND)
ED4A	ADC	HL,BC	FDCB054E	BIT	1,(IY+IND)
ED5A	ADC	HL,DE	CB4F	BIT	1,A
ED6A	ADC	HL,HL	CB48	BIT	1,B
ED7A	ADC	HL,SP	CB49	BIT	1,C
86	ADD	A,(HL)	CB4A	BIT	1,D
DD8605	ADD	A,(IX+IND)	CB4B	BIT	1,E
FD8605	ADD	A,(IY+IND)	CB4C	BIT	1,H
87	ADD	A,A	CB4D	BIT	1,L
80	ADD	A,B	CB56	BIT	2,(HL)
81	ADD	A,C	DDCB0556	BIT	2,(IX+IND)
82	ADD	A,D	FDCB0556	BIT	2,(IY+IND)
83	ADD	A,E	CB57	BIT	2,A
84	ADD	A,H	CB50	BIT	2,B
85	ADD	A,L	CB51	BIT	2,C
C620	ADD	A,N	CB52	BIT	2,D
09	ADD	HL,BC	CB53	BIT	2,E
19	ADD	HL,DE	CB54	BIT	2,H
29	ADD	HL,HL	CB55	BIT	2,L
39	ADD	HL,SP	CB5E	BIT	3,(HL)
DD09	ADD	IX,BC	DDCB055E	BIT	3,(IX+IND)
DD19	ADD	IX,DE	FDCB055E	BIT	3,(IY+IND)
DD29	ADD	IX,IX	CB5F	BIT	3,A
DD39	ADD	IX,SP	CB58	BIT	3,B
FD09	ADD	IY,BC	CB59	BIT	3,C
FD19	ADD	IY,DE	CB5A	BIT	3,D
FD29	ADD	IY,IY	CB5B	BIT	3,E
FD39	ADD	IY,SP	CB5C	BIT	3,H
A6	AND	(HL)	CB5D	BIT	3,L
DDA605	AND	(IX+IND)	CB66	BIT	4,(HL)
FDA605	AND	(IY+IND)	DDCB0566	BIT	4,(IX+IND)
A7	AND	A	FDCB0566	BIT	4,(IY+IND)
A0	AND	B	CB67	BIT	4,A
A1	AND	C	CB60	BIT	4,B
A2	AND	D	CB61	BIT	4,C
A3	AND	E	CB62	BIT	4,D
A4	AND	H	CB63	BIT	4,E
A5	AND	L	CB64	BIT	4,H
E620	AND	N	CB65	BIT	4,L
CB46	BIT	0,(HL)	CB6E	BIT	5,(HL)

OBJECT CODE	SOURCE STATEMENT		OBJECT CODE	SOURCE STATEMENT	
DDCB056E	BIT	5,(IX+IND)	EDA9	CPD	
FDCB056E	BIT	5,(IY+IND)	EDB9	CPDR	
CB6F	BIT	5,A	EDA1	CPL	
CB68	BIT	5,B	EDB1	CPIR	
CB69	BIT	5,C	2F	CPL	
CB6A	BIT	5,D	27	DAA	
CB6B	BIT	5,E	35	DEC	(HL)
CB6C	BIT	5,H	DD3505	DEC	(IX+IND)
CB6D	BIT	5,L	FD3505	DEC	(IY+IND)
CB76	BIT	6,(HL)	3D	DEC	A
DDCB0576	BIT	6,(IX+IND)	05	DEC	B
FDCB0576	BIT	6,(IY+IND)	0B	DEC	BC
CB77	BIT	6,A	0D	DEC	C
CB70	BIT	6,B	15	DEC	D
CB71	BIT	6,C	1B	DEC	DE
CB72	BIT	6,D	1D	DEC	E
CB73	BIT	6,E	25	DEC	H
CB74	BIT	6,H	2B	DEC	HL
CB75	BIT	6,L	DD2B	DEC	IX
CB7E	BIT	7,(HL)	FD2B	DEC	IY
DDCB057E	BIT	7,(IX+IND)	2D	DEC	L
FDCB057E	BIT	7,(IY+IND)	3B	DEC	SP
CB7F	BIT	7,A	F3	DI	
CB78	BIT	7,B	102E	DJNZ	DIS
CB79	BIT	7,C	FB	EI	
CB7A	BIT	7,D	E3	EX	(SP),HL
CB7B	BIT	7,E	DDE3	EX	(SP),IX
CB7C	BIT	7,H	FDE3	EX	(SP),IY
CB7D	BIT	7,L	08	EX	AF,AF'
DC8405	CALL	C,NN	EB	EX	DE,HL
FC8405	CALL	M,NN	D9	EXX	
D48405	CALL	NC,NN	76	HALT	
CD8405	CALL	NN	ED46	IM	0
C48405	CALL	NZ,NN	ED56	IM	1
F48405	CALL	P,NN	ED5E	IM	2
EC8405	CALL	PE,NN	ED78	IN	A,(C)
E48405	CALL	PO,NN	DB20	IN	A,N
CC8405	CALL	Z,NN	ED40	IN	B,(C)
3F	CCF		ED48	IN	C,(C)
8E	CP	(HL)	ED50	IN	D,(C)
DD8E05	CP	(IX+IND)	ED58	IN	E,(C)
FD8E05	CP	(IY+IND)	ED60	IN	H,(C)
BF	CP	A	ED68	IN	L,(C)
B8	CP	B	34	INC	(HL)
B9	CP	C	DD3405	INC	(IX+IND)
BA	CP	D	FD3405	INC	(IY+IND)
BB	CP	E	3C	INC	A
BC	CP	H	04	INC	B
BD	CP	L	03	INC	BC
FE20	CP	N	0C	INC	C

OBJECT CODE	SOURCE STATEMENT		OBJECT CODE	SOURCE STATEMENT	
14	INC	D	FD7105	LD	(IY+IND),C
13	INC	DE	FD7205	LD	(IY+IND),D
1C	INC	E	FD7305	LD	(IY+IND),E
24	INC	H	FD7405	LD	(IY+IND),H
23	INC	HL	FD7505	LD	(IY+IND),L
DD23	INC	IX	FD360520	LD	(IY+IND),N
FD23	INC	IY	328405	LD	(NN),A
2C	INC	L	ED438405	LD	(NN),BC
33	INC	SP	ED538405	LD	(NN),DE
EDAA	IND		228405	LD	(NN),HL
EDBA	INDR		DD228405	LD	(NN),IX
EDA2	INI		FD228405	LD	(NN),IY
EDB2	INIR		ED738405	LD	(NN),SP
E9	JP	(HL)	0A	LD	A,(BC)
DDE9	JP	(IX)	1A	LD	A,(DE)
FDE9	JP	(IY)	7E	LD	A,(HL)
DA8405	JP	C,NN	DD7E05	LD	A,(IX+IND)
FA8405	JP	M,NN	FD7E05	LD	A,(IY+IND)
D28405	JP	NC,NN	3A8405	LD	A,(NN)
C38405	JP	NN	7F	LD	A,A
C28405	JP	NZ,NN	78	LD	A,B
F28405	JP	P,NN	79	LD	A,C
EA8405	JP	PE,NN	7A	LD	A,D
E28405	JP	PO,NN	7B	LD	A,E
CA8405	JP	Z,NN	7C	LD	A,H
382E	JR	DIS	ED57	LD	A,I
302E	JR	NC,DIS	7D	LD	A,L
202E	JR	NZ,DIS	3E20	LD	A,N
282E	JR	Z,DIS	46	LD	B,(HL)
02	LD	(BC),A	DD4605	LD	B,(IX+IND)
12	LD	(DE),A	FD4605	LD	B,(IY+IND)
77	LD	(HL),A	47	LD	B,A
70	LD	(HL),B	40	LD	B,B
71	LD	(HL),C	41	LD	B,C
72	LD	(HL),D	42	LD	B,D
73	LD	(HL),E	43	LD	B,E
74	LD	(HL),H	44	LD	D,H
75	LD	(HL),L	45	LD	D,L
3620	LD	(HL),N	0620	LD	B,N
DD7705	LD	(IX+IND),A	ED4B8405	LD	BC,(NN)
DD7005	LD	(IX+IND),B	018405	LD	BC,NN
DD7105	LD	(IX+IND),C	4E	LD	C,(HL)
DD7205	LD	(IX+IND),D	DD4E05	LD	C,(IX+IND)
DD7305	LD	(IX+IND),E	FD4E05	LD	C,(IY+IND)
DD7405	LD	(IX+IND),H	4F	LD	C,A
DD7505	LD	(IX+IND),L	48	LD	C,B
DD360520	LD	(IX+IND),N	49	LD	C,C
FD7705	LD	(IY+IND),A	4A	LD	C,D
FD7005	LD	(IY+IND),B	4B	LD	C,E

OBJECT CODE	SOURCE STATEMENT		OBJECT CODE	SOURCE STATEMENT	
4D	LD	C,L	6A	LD	L,D
0E20	LD	C,N	6B	LD	L,E
56	LD	D,(HL)	6C	LD	L,H
DD5605	LD	D,(IX+IND)	6D	LD	L,L
FD5605	LD	D,(IY+IND)	2E20	LD	L,N
57	LD	D,A	ED7B8405	LD	SP,(NN)
50	LD	D,B	F9	LD	SP,HL
51	LD	D,C	DDF9	LD	SP,IX
52	LD	D,D	FDF9	LD	SP,IY
53	LD	D,E	318405	LD	SP,NN
54	LD	D,H	EDA8	LDD	
55	LD	D,L	EDB8	LDDR	
1620	LD	D,N	EDA0	LDI	
ED5B8405	LD	DE,(NN)	EDB0	LDIR	
118405	LD	DE,NN	ED44	NEG	
5E	LD	E,(HL)	00	NOP	
DD5E05	LD	E,(IX+IND)	B6	OR	(HL)
FD5E05	LD	E,(IY+IND)	DDB605	OR	(IX+IND)
5F	LD	E,A	FDB605	OR	(IY+IND)
58	LD	E,B	B7	OR	A
59	LD	E,C	B0	OR	B
5A	LD	E,D	B1	OR	C
5B	LD	E,E	B2	OR	D
5C	LD	E,H	B3	OR	E
5D	LD	E,L	B4	OR	H
1E20	LD	E,N	B5	OR	L
66	LD	H,(HL)	F620	OR	N
DD6605	LD	H,(IX+IND)	EDBB	OTDR	
FD6605	LD	H,(IY+IND)	EDB3	OTIR	
67	LD	H,A	ED79	OUT	(C),A
60	LD	H,B	ED41	OUT	(C),B
61	LD	H,C	ED49	OUT	(C),C
62	LD	H,D	ED51	OUT	(C),D
63	LD	H,E	ED59	OUT	(C),E
64	LD	H,H	ED61	OUT	(C),H
65	LD	H,L	ED69	OUT	(C),L
2620	LD	H,N	D320	OUT	N,A
2A8405	LD	HL,(NN)	EDAB	OUTD	
218405	LD	HL,NN	EDA3	OUTI	
ED47	LD	I,A	F1	POP	AF
DD2A8405	LD	IX,(NN)	C1	POP	BC
DD218405	LD	IX,NN	D1	POP	DE
FD2A8405	LD	IY,(NN)	E1	POP	HL
FD218405	LD	IY,NN	DDE1	POP	IX
6E	LD	L,(HL)	FDE1	POP	IY
DD6E05	LD	L,(IX+IND)	F5	PUSH	AF
FD6E05	LD	L,(IY+IND)	C5	PUSH	BC
6F	LD	L,A	D5	PUSH	DE
68	LD	L,B	E5	PUSH	HL
69	LD	L,C	DDE5	PUSH	IX

OBJECT CODE	SOURCE STATEMENT		OBJECT CODE	SOURCE STATEMENT	
FDE5	PUSH	IY	CBA5	RES	4,L
CB86	RES	0,(HL)	CBAE	RES	5,(HL)
DDCB0586	RES	0,(IX+IND)	DDCB05AE	RES	5,(IX+IND)
FDCB0596	RES	0,(IY+IND)	FDCB05AE	RES	5,(IY+IND)
CB87	RES	0,A	CBAF	RES	5,A
CB80	RES	0,B	CBA8	RES	5,B
CB81	RES	0,C	CBA9	RES	5,C
CB82	RES	0,D	CBAA	RES	5,D
CB83	RES	0,E	CBAB	RES	5,E
CB84	RES	0,H	CBAC	RES	5,H
CB85	RES	0,L	CBAD	RES	5,L
CB8E	RES	1,(HL)	CBB6	RES	6,(HL)
DDCB058E	RES	1,(IX+IND)	DDCB05B6	RES	6,(IX+IND)
FDCB058E	RES	1,(IY+IND)	FDCB05B6	RES	6,(IY+IND)
CB8F	RES	1,A	CBB7	RES	6,A
CB88	RES	1,B	CBB0	RES	6,B
CB89	RES	1,C	CBB1	RES	6,C
CB8A	RES	1,D	CBB2	RES	6,D
CB8B	RES	1,E	CBB3	RES	6,E
CB8C	RES	1,H	CBB4	RES	6,H
CB8D	RES	1,L	CBB5	RES	6,L
CB96	RES	2,(HL)	CBBE	RES	7,(HL)
DDCB0596	RES	2,(IX+IND)	DDCB05BE	RES	7,(IX+IND)
FDCB0596	RES	2,(IY+IND)	FDCB05BE	RES	7,(IY+IND)
CB97	RES	2,A	CBBF	RES	7,A
CB90	RES	2,B	CBB8	RES	7,B
CB91	RES	2,C	CBB9	RES	7,C
CB92	RES	2,D	CBBA	RES	7,D
CB93	RES	2,E	CBBB	RES	7,E
CB94	RES	2,H	CBBC	RES	7,H
CB95	RES	2,L	CBBD	RES	7,L
CB9E	RES	3,(HL)	C9	RET	
DDCB059E	RES	3,(IX+IND)	D8	RET	C
FDCB059E	RES	3,(IY+IND)	F8	RET	M
CB9F	RES	3,A	D0	RET	NC
CB98	RES	3,B	C0	RET	NZ
CB99	RES	3,C	F0	RET	P
CB9A	RES	3,D	E8	RET	PE
CB9B	RES	3,E	E0	RET	PO
CB9C	RES	3,H	C8	RET	Z
CB9D	RES	3,L	ED4D	RETI	
CBA6	RES	4,(HL)	ED45	RETN	
DDCB05A6	RES	4,(IX+IND)	CB16	RL	(HL)
FDCB05A6	RES	4,(IY+IND)	DDCB0516	RL	(IX+IND)
CBA7	RES	4,A	FDCB0516	RL	(IY+IND)
CBA0	RES	4,B	CB17	RL	A
CBA1	RES	4,C	CB10	RL	B
CBA2	RES	4,D	CB11	RL	C
CBA3	RES	4,E	CB12	RL	D
CBA4	RES	4,H	CB13	RL	E

OBJECT CODE	SOURCE STATEMENT		OBJECT CODE	SOURCE STATEMENT	
CB14	RL	H	98	SBC	A,B
CB15	RL	L	99	SBC	A,C
17	RLA		9A	SBC	A,D
CBØ6	RLC	(HL)	9B	SBC	A,E
DDCBØ5Ø6	RLC	(IX+IND)	9C	SBC	A,H
FDCBØ5Ø6	RLC	(IY+IND)	9D	SBC	A,L
CBØ7	RLC	A	DE2Ø	SBC	A,N
CBØØ	RLC	B	ED42	SBC	HL,BC
CBØ1	RLC	C	ED52	SBC	HL,DE
CBØ2	RLC	D	ED62	SBC	HL,HL
CBØ3	RLC	E	ED72	SBC	HL,SP
CBØ4	RLC	H	37	SCF	
CBØ5	RLC	L	CBC6	SET	0,(HL)
Ø7	RLCA		DDCBØ5C6	SET	0,(IX+IND)
ED6F	RLD		FDCBØ5C6	SET	0,(IY+IND)
CB1E	RR	(HL)	CBC7	SET	0,A
DDCBØ51E	RR	(IX+IND)	CBCØ	SET	0,B
FDCBØ51E	RR	(IY+IND)	CBC1	SET	0,C
CB1F	RR	A	CBC2	SET	0,D
CB18	RR	B	CBC3	SET	0,E
CB19	RR	C	CBC4	SET	0,H
CB1A	RR	D	CBC5	SET	0,L
CB1B	RR	E	CBCE	SET	1,(HL)
CB1C	RR	H	DDCBØ5CE	SET	1,(IX+IND)
CB1D	RR	L	FDCBØ5CE	SET	1,(IY+IND)
1F	RRA		CBCF	SET	1,A
CBØE	RRC	(HL)	CBC8	SET	1,B
DDCBØ5ØE	RRC	(IX+IND)	CBC9	SET	1,C
FDCBØ5ØE	RRC	(IY+IND)	CBCA	SET	1,D
CBØF	RRC	A	CBCB	SET	1,E
CBØ8	RRC	B	CBCC	SET	1,H
CBØ9	RRC	C	CBCD	SET	1,L
CBØA	RRC	D	CBD6	SET	2,(HL)
CBØB	RRC	E	DDCBØ5D6	SET	2,(IX+IND)
CBØC	RRC	H	FDCBØ5D6	SET	2,(IY+ID)
CBØD	RRC	L	CBD7	SET	2,A
ØF	RRCA		CBDØ	SET	2,B
ED67	RRD		CBD1	SET	2,C
C7	RST	Ø	CBD2	SET	2,D
CF	RST	Ø8H	CBD3	SET	2,E
D7	RST	10H	CBD4	SET	2,H
DF	RST	18H	CBD5	SET	2,L
E7	RST	20H	CBDE	SET	3,(HL)
EF	RST	28H	DDCBØ5DE	SET	3,(IX+IND)
F7	RST	30H	FDCBØ5DE	SET	3,(IY+IND)
FF	RST	38H	CBDF	SET	3,A
9E	SBC	A,(HL)	CBD8	SET	3,B
DD9EØ5	SBC	A,(IX+IND)	CBD9	SET	3,C
FD9EØ5	SBC	A,(IY+IND)	CBDA	SET	3,D
9F	SBC	A,A	CBDB	SET	3,E

OBJECT CODE	SOURCE STATEMENT		OBJECT CODE	SOURCE STATEMENT	
CBDC	SET	3,H	CB24	SLA	H
CBDD	SET	3,L	CB25	SLA	L
CBE6	SET	4,(HL)	CB2E	SRA	(HL)
DDCB05E6	SET	4,(IX+IND)	DDCB052E	SRA	(IX+IND)
FDCB05E6	SET	4,(IY+IND)	FDCB052E	SRA	(IY+IND)
CBE7	SET	4,A	CB2F	SRA	A
CBE0	SET	4,B	CB28	SRA	B
CBE1	SET	4,C	CB29	SRA	C
CBE2	SET	4,D	CB2A	SRA	D
CBE3	SET	4,E	CB2B	SRA	E
CBE4	SET	4,H	CB2C	SRA	H
CBE5	SET	4,L	CB2D	SRA	L
CBEE	SET	5,(HL)	CB3E	SRL	(HL)
DDCB05EE	SET	5,(IX+IND)	DDCB053E	SRL	(IX+IND)
FDCB05EE	SET	5,(IY+IND)	FDCB053E	SRL	(IY+IND)
CBEF	SET	5,A	CB3F	SRL	A
CBE8	SET	5,B	CB38	SRL	B
CBE9	SET	5,C	CB39	SRL	C
CBEA	SET	5,D	CB3A	SRL	D
CBEB	SET	5,E	CB3B	SRL	E
CBEC	SET	5,H	CB3C	SRL	H
CBED	SET	5,L	CB3D	SRL	L
CBF6	SET	6,(HL)	96	SUB	(HL)
DDCB05F6	SET	6,(IX+IND)	DD9605	SUB	(IX+IND)
FDCB05F6	SET	6,(IY+IND)	FD9605	SUB	(IY+IND)
CBF7	SET	6,A	97	SUB	A
CBF0	SET	6,B	90	SUB	B
CBF1	SET	6,C	91	SUB	C
CBF2	SET	6,D	92	SUB	D
CBF3	SET	6,E	93	SUB	E
CBF4	SET	6,H	94	SUB	H
CBF5	SET	6,L	95	SUB	L
CBFE	SET	7,(HL)	D620	SUB	N
DDCB05FE	SET	7,(IX+IND)	AE	XOR	(HL)
FDCB05FE	SET	7,(IY+IND)	DDAE05	XOR	(IX+IND)
CBFF	SET	7,A	FDAE05	XOR	(IY+IND)
CBF8	SET	7,B	AF	XOR	A
CBF9	SET	7,C	A8	XOR	B
CBFA	SET	7,D	A9	XOR	C
CBFB	SET	7,E	AA	XOR	D
CBFC	SET	7,H	AB	XOR	E
CBFD	SET	7,L	AC	XOR	H
CB26	SLA	(HL)	AD	XOR	L
DDCB0526	SLA	(IX+IND)	EE20	XOR	N
FDCB0526	SLA	(IY+IND)			
CB27	SLA	A			
CB20	SLA	B			
CB21	SLA	C			
CB22	SLA	D			
CB23	SLA	E			

Appendix E: Selected Bibliography

Radio Shack Reference Manuals:

LEVEL II BASIC REFERENCE MANUAL.

TRSDOS & DISK BASIC REFERENCE MANUAL (Catalog Number 26-2104).

EDITOR/ASSEMBLER USER INSTRUCTION MANUAL (Catalog Number 26-2002).

Above are all published by Radio Shack, a division of Tandy Corporation, Fort Worth, Texas 76102.

Z-80 Assembly-language programming:

TRS-80 ASSEMBLY-LANGUAGE PROGRAMMING by William Barden, Jr. Published by Radio Shack (Catalog Number 62-2006).

THE Z-80 MICROCOMPUTER HANDBOOK by William Barden, Jr. Howard W. Sams & Co., Inc., 4300 West 62nd Street, Indianapolis, Indiana 46268.

PRACTICAL MICROCOMPUTER PROGRAMMING: THE Z80 by W. J. Weller. Northern Technology Books, Box 62, Evanston, Illinois 60204.

TRS-80 technical information:

MICRO APPLICATIONS TRS-80 DISC INTERFACING GUIDE by William Barden, Jr. Micro Applications, 24232 Tahoe Court, Laguna Niguel, California 92677.

TRS-80 DISK & OTHER MYSTERIES by H. C. Pennington. Published by IJG Inc., 569 North Mountain Avenue, Upland, California 91786.

TRS-80 SUPERMAP by Fuller Software, 630 East Springdale, Grand Prairie, Texas 75051.

DISASSEMBLED HANDBOOK FOR TRS-80 (two volumes). Richcraft Engineering Ltd., Drawer 1065, Chautauqua, New York 14722.